AF291118

Gino Leineweber (Ed.)

# Songs from the Wind

## International Poetry

Verlag Expeditionen

Publisher: Verlag Expeditionen, 2023
Gino Leineweber (Ed.)
Songs from the Wind
International Poetry

Printed in Germany

Cover Design Angela Schwarze, Germany
Foto "A Dandelion" by Dreamstime.com
ISBN 978-3-947911-92-9

# Poetry from


Prologue ............................................................ 11
Christopher Okemwa, Kenya ............................... 15
Achim Amme, Germany ....................................... 18
Agron Shele, Albanian/Belgium ........................... 20
Albrecht Classen, USA/Germany .......................... 24
Ali Al Hazmi, Saudi Arabia .................................. 28
Alicja Kuberska, Poland ...................................... 34
Anna Würth, Germany ......................................... 36
Annabel Villar, Uruguay/Spain ............................ 40
Antje Stehn, Germany ......................................... 44
Aristea Papalexandrou, Greece .......................... 46
Ayeshah Émon, Planet Earth ............................... 48
Barry Stevenson, UK/Germany ............................ 52
Betty Gilmore, USA ............................................ 54
Bill Wolak, USA ................................................. 56
Chloe Koutsoubelli, Greece ................................ 58
Claudia Piccinno, Italy ....................................... 60
Daniel Calabrese, Argentina ............................... 64
Dimitris P. Kraniotis, Greece .............................. 66
Don Krieger, USA .............................................. 68
Dorel Cosma, Romania ...................................... 70
Elçin Sevgi Suçin, Turkey ................................... 78
Emel Koşar, Turkey ............................................ 80
Emina Čabaravdić-Kamber, Bosnia ..................... 82
George Wallace, USA ......................................... 84
Gino Leineweber, Germany/Italy ......................... 88
Hussein Habasch, Kurdistan ............................... 90
Hema Ravi, India ............................................... 91
Hilal Karahan, Turkey ......................................... 94
Holly Iglesias, USA ............................................ 96

Janine Troutman, Germany     98
Jenny Lkhagvasuren, Mongolia     102
Jeton Kelmendi, Belgium/Kosovo     104
Julio Pavanetti, Uruguay/Spain     110
Kirsten Doebler, Germany     114
Liana Sakelliou, Greece     118
Lily Exarchopoulou, Greece     120
Maja Herman, Serbia/USA     122
Maren Schönfeld, Germany     124
Margret Silvester, Germany     126
Maria Miraglia, Italy     128
Merita Paparisto, Albania/Canada     130
Mesut Şenol, Turkey     132
Metin Turan, Turkey     134
Michael Speier, Germany     138
Milica Jeftimijević Lilić, Serbia     140
Muberra Karamanoglu, Turkey     144
Neelam Saxena Chandra, India     146
Padmaja Iyengar-Paddy, India     148
Raed Anis Al-Jishi, Saudi Arabia     152
Reshma Ramesh, India     154
Sitawa Namwalie, Kenya     156
Susanna Piontek, USA/Germany     160
Utz Rachowski, Germany     164
Uwe Friesel, Germany     168
Varsha Das, India     170
Yiorgos Chouliaras, Greece     173
Yuray Tolentino Hevia, Cuba     174
Zorin Diaconescu, Romania     176
Biographies     178

Gino Leineweber (Ed.)

# Songs from the Wind

International Poetry

# Prologue

These days, when the world once again seems to be staggering on the brink of disaster, 60 poets from 22 countries and four continents are using poetry to try to bring some light into the darkness.

It is the fifth anthology published by the German publisher Verlag Expeditionen. The last four were about the seasons, and this book is about one of the elements, the wind.

However, it's not only one of the classic four elements because the wind is the archetype of movement and, therefore, the essence of time and space and shows us life's core.

In 1937, German poets and composers Bruno Balz and Lothar Brühne announced: "Der Wind hat mir ein Lied erzählt" (The Wind Has Told Me A Song).

The wind had told the song for the romantic movie *La Habanera*, sung by the Swedish actress and singer Zarah Leander. The lyrics are about loneliness, longing, and hope. The main character listens to the wind, which tells her of an ineffable, beautiful happiness. The wind symbolizes the connection to nature and the world around us.

Like the soundtrack that leads to metaphorical excursions, the idea of the element's movements runs in the blood of poets. Therefore, we'll find songs of the wind in numerous examples from the beginning of poetry writing until the publication of this international anthology. You will find loneliness, longing, and hope again. You will find them from different cultural backgrounds. You will find them in the fine art of poetry.

I know the poets in this book, who submitted their poems, from several worldwide poetry festivals or collaborated on different poetry projects. So, I know their gifted voice, profound thoughts, and style. The result of this can be seen in over sixty significant poems. The poems in this book are published in the poet's native language and American English.

I am grateful to my friends and colleagues and wish the readers joy and delight with this volume of poetry.

Gino Leineweber (Ed.)
Vietri Sul Mare, Italy,
November 20, 2023

There are always waves on the water.
Sometimes they are big, sometimes they are small,
and sometimes they are almost imperceptible.
The water's waves are churned up by the winds,
which come and go and vary in direction and intensity,
just as do the winds of stress and change in our lives,
which stir up the waves in our minds."

Jon Kabat-Zinn
Wherever You Go, There You Are

THE WIND I
*Christopher Okemwa, Kenya*

The soft, fragile wind of life
blows you in and out,
everywhere and anywhere
mournfully, by and by
through the dark woods
deep-seated seas, endless spaces
you delicately hold onto its wings
with hope and optimism
anticipation and desire
waiting for the flicker of light
the red ray of sunlight after dawn
or a bird's exultant song
that drops in as a harbinger
of life's pure abundance
or a gentle shower of rain
to serve as a divine blessing
or a cluster of falling stars
that gather on your open palms;
the wind of life, empty and aimless
blows and blows, in and out
everywhere and anywhere
plunging you into an abyss of darkness
leaving behind a residuum of consciousness!
your own consciousness
that stay hanging on for a while
maybe for long
maybe forever.

THE WIND II
*Christopher Okemwa, Kenya*

I hear you singing, swishing
and wheezing in every direction
shaking and blowing off thatch-
roofs from huts in dereliction

Squeezing through a dense bush
forest, newly-cut hedgerow
raging all the way, settling in
a dark glade with a blazing row

You lift confetti, festoon, and old
sacks, scattering them in the sky
you then pick light clothes from
the line as you whine and cry

Hurling them on tarmac roads
paths, bushes, and fields afar
flutters and whirrs about fuzzy flags,
spiraling up fluffs and fur

You enter our bedroom through an
open creaking window on the wall
disrupts mosquito nets and windows-
swags in your mischievous prowl

16

Rumples blankets and bed sheets,
stirring crockery on the bedside table
leaving the room with a tremble,
a whine and a soft danceable treble

Sometimes, you waft along silently,
swallowing your anger and pride
listening, one might think you have
dropped down, fainted, and died

But suddenly, the leaves outside go
nodding, fluttering, and fidgeting
then one realizes that you are alive,
whistling a tune that is riveting

In gusts, you are always back
with gusto, grumbling among trees
gurgling through thick hedgerows;
a guiro, whining and rumbling

Gratuitous, leaving behind broken
boughs, scattered twigs, and foliage
telling of your wreaking power,
a mighty fury, a flaunting proud rage.

# DER WIND SINGT IN DEN ZWEIGEN
*Achim Amme, Deutschland*

18

> Denk an nichtige Dinge,
> denk an den Wind.
> *Truman Capote*

Der Wind singt in den Zweigen
von unerhörten Fernen.
Er will wohl damit zeigen,
es gibt noch viel zu lernen,

von Dingen, die wir ahnen,
nicht kennen oder wissen
und uns daran gemahnen,
was wir noch lernen müssen.

Vielleicht ist, was geschieht,
jedoch ganz anders, und
der Wind singt nur ein Lied
und tut uns gar nichts kund.

# THE WIND SINGS IN THE BRANCHES
*Achim Amme, Germany*
*Translated by Birgit Funk, Germany*

> Think of nothing things,
> think of wind.
> *Truman Capote*

The wind sings in the branches
of faraway distances.
Perhaps it wants to show
there's still so much to know

'bout things, we only guess
but cannot grasp, but, yes,
they do remind us such
there's still to learn so much.

What's happening may be
a dazzling fantasy.
The wind just sings a song
saying nothing but: So long!

ZAMBAKU NË LIQEN
*Agron Shele, Albanian/Belgium*


Çuditem më the:
si nuk e ndjen pëhere të njëjtën aromë parfurmi *Dior*
në vjeshtë dhe në dimër,
kur natyra zhvishet dhe pemët ndjejënë të ftohtin në
asht
në shpirt dhe trup
me dëshira të fshehura
dhe shpresës se lulëzimi do të vijë tjetër stinë.

Çuditem dhe më shumë
kur kaloj fare pranë teje e ti s' më shikon,
por harron se murgu ka kohë që shikon vetëm
manastirin
dhe tek qiparisi i tij sytë i gozhdon.

E ç' duhet me shumë
se një pejgamber i hapur
dhe një plegrin që kohën e pakohë zbulon
në fshikulla të fshehta dhimbje
dhe shenja që me trupin në dhe' do i çojë..

Pastaj s' mund të harroj
se si koketën e mbledhur e lëshove përfund,
si një sharm të ethes së mëkatit
dhe një drithme që përshkon marrëzisht.

Ti arrite gjer tek mua
shelg u bëre dhe u përkule gjer në dhe,
ndërsa parfumi ndiqte bukurinë e trazuar bordurave të
njohura
në një fluturim të bardhë që ngjitej përmbi re.

Ti fole shumë e më shumë
për Orkidet gjithësesi
lule të çelura në sytë e një gruaje
dhe zambakë të prehur kaq qetë mbi një liqen.

THE LILY OF THE LAKE
*Agron Shele, Albanian/Belgium*
*Translated by Merita Paparisto, Albania/Canada*

I'm amazed—you said
How could you not always sense the same perfume's
aroma, *Dior*
In autumn and winter?
When the scenery is stripped, and trees feel cold to the
bones
In body and soul
With their hidden desires
And the hope that blossoms are coming in yet another
season.

I'm even more amazed
When I pass you by, and you don't realize me
Forgetting that for a very long time
the monk has only seen the monastery
and at his cypress, he pierces his eyes.

What more could you need
Then, an open prophet
Or a pilgrim that reveals timelessness
On the hidden whips of sorrow
And scars on his body that will pass on with him.

I cannot forget as well, how you unwrapped
The crouching coquette
Like a charm of the fever of sin
Overcoming with trembling madness

You reached for me
Became a willow bending to the earth
Whereas the perfume followed the troubled beauty
To the known walkways
In a white flight, capturing the clouds.

You talked and talked
about orchids
the flowers that bloomed in a woman's eyes
and the lilies that quietly doze on the lake's surface.

## WIND OH WIND
*Albrecht Classen, USA*


„… und auf den Fluren lass die Winde los",
sprach der große Dichter,
und so lass ich, ganz nach Bedarf,
meine Worte los, um über die Lande
hin zu treiben, frei und unbeschwert.

Wie im Traume wirbeln mich die Winde
durch die Wattewolken hinweg,
zupfen an den Haaren und zerren an den Schößen,
drehen mich um und um hoch in der Luft,
ich vergnüg' mich am Spaß ganz frei dort oben.

Wie viele Länder haben nicht die Winde,
und wie viele Menschen erst gar
bereist und geduckt, durchgerüttelt und geschubst!
Erst kommt der Sturm und dann der Regen,
ich rieche es im Wind und fühle die Tropfen.

Die Bäume trifft der Sturm mit aller Macht,
wie beugt sich der bebende Wald!
Wie ducken wir uns nicht alle,
der Wind, der Wind, das himmlische Kind,
es toben die Atmosphären, es dröhnt die Luft.

Staub und Pollen, Sand und Samen, Blüten und Duft
treiben dahin, flugs im Flug, hurtig mein Kind,
ein lustiger Geselle, ein bärbeißiger Greis,
ein bitterer Sturm, ein kühles Lüftchen,
alles bewegt sich und fliegt im Wind davon.

Hitze für die einen, Kälte für die anderen,
Luftbewegungen ruhig und stürmisch,
tobend in der Stratosphäre,
von der Sahara gen Norden,
von den Alpenhöhen hinab in das Tal.

Schicksalsschläge, der Wind kennt sie schon,
Geburt und Tod, luftbewegt,
wogende Weizenfelder,
Wellen windgepeitscht,
und tief beugt sich die ganze Welt.

Nimm mich mit auf deinen Wegen,
kühler Wind aus alten Tagen,
lass uns die Augen brennen
in den heißen Zeiten,
ein würdiger Geselle oder bloß Pustekuchen.

## WIND OH WIND
*Albrecht Classen, USA*

"…in the fields release the winds",
said the great poet,
so I let, just as the need calls for it,
go of my words to make them float
across the land, free and unhampered.

The winds toss me around as if in a dream
across the clouds of cotton,
they plug at my hair and pull at my shirt tails,
they turn me around and around high in the air,
and I have fun with it, so free up there.

So many countries have the winds
and so many people have they
visited and pushed down, shaken up and bumped up!
First, there is the storm, and then comes the rain,
I smell it in the wind and feel the drops.

The storm hits the trees with full force,
see how the trembling forest bends down!
we all have to bow down our heads,
it is the wind, the wind, the heavenly child,
the atmosphere rages, the air is roaring.

Dust and pollen, sand and seeds, blossoms and smell
float along, fast flying, come quickly along, my child,
a funny fellow, a grim-looking old man,
a cool little wind, a biting storm,
everything moves forward and flies away in the wind.

Heat for some, coldness for others,
movement of the air, calm and stormy,
raging in the stratosphere,
from the Sahara toward the north,
from the Alpine heights down into the valley.

Strikes of fortune, the wind knows them all,
birth and death, moved by air,
heaving fields of wheat,
waves whipped by the wind,
and the entire world bends down so deeply.

Take me with you on your journey,
cool wind from the old days,
let us burn the eyes
during the hot season,
dignified fellow, or only puffy cake?

**خُذني إلى جسدي**
علي الحازمي ، السعودية


قالت امرأةٌ للمسافرِ : خُذْني إلى البحر ،
هُناك ولدتُ على شغفِ الموج
تَحمِلني الريحُ في رحلةٍ
لم أَعُدْ أتذكّرُ منها سوى غُربةٍ
تتناسلُ في قَفْرِ رُوحي ،
لم تَعُدْ حَاجتي للقليلِ من الحظِّ
تُسْعِفُني بالمزيدِ من الصبرِ
كيما أُقَلِّبَ جمرَ انتظاري الطويل




يقولُ فَتىً لفتاةٍ تَدُسُّ أَنامِلَها
تَحت أزرارِ سُترتِهِ بانهمارٍ :
دَعي رَغْبَتي في خِضَمِّكِ
تطفو قليلاً على صفحةِ الماءِ ،
فالبحرُ يُهْدِرُ فُرْصَتَنا
في اللَّواذِ بطوقِ حنينٍ نَسَجْنَا
مُوشَّحَهُ في ليالٍ بهيجة ،
عَانِقيني طويلاً فإنَّ العِنَاقَ يُهَدْهِدُ
حُرْقَتَنا في انتظارِ البعيد ،
دَعي شَمْعَتي في غِيابيَ مُطفأةً وأَنيري
بتوقِ المُحبينَ عتمةَ هذا المسَاء ،
كان يعلمُ
أنَّ السماءَ ستُمْطِرُ ثانيةً
في غيابِ يديهِ ... ولم ينتظرْ !



ـ أخَافُ من البحر ...
ـ تَخَافينَ مِثْلي من البحر ؟!

والبحرُ نَايُ الطبيعةِ ، سَهلُ الحنينِ ،
مَلاذُ الوجود !
ـ أَخَافُ عَليكَ من البحرِ ، من ضِفَّةٍ
تتآكلُ من تَحتِ أقدامِهِ في جميعِ الفصول
سنتعبُ ، قُلتُ لكَ الأمس :
خُذْني إلى جَسَدي ... نستريح !
سنتعبُ ، إنْ أمطرتْنا السواحلُ
بالعطشِ المتهافتِ في صمتِها ،
سنتعبُ ، إنْ سَيَّجَتْنا المسافةُ
بالضّجرِ المعدنيّ ، وصارَ لنا الحُلمُ
أَبعدَ من كَرْمَةٍ في اليَدين


بحارةٌ يسألونَ عن البحر !
كَيف لهم أنْ يعودوا إلى مِلحِهِ
بعدَ تِلكَ السنين !
ماذا تَبقَّى لهم في مِيَاهِهِ
غَيْرُ التماعِ الطحالبِ والتعبِ المُرّ ؟!


الأقَاصي التي بَدَّدَتْ سَعْيَهم
بانكسارِ مجاديفِ رغبتِهم
لم تَعُدْ تلتفتْ
لحرائقِ أحداقِهم كُلَّمَا سأَلُوهَا
عن الريح : ماذا أرادتْ
بتحريكِ دَفَّةِ أسفارِهم باتجاهِ الضّنى ؟

يخسرُ الذاهبونَ إلى البحرِ
كُلَّ لآلئ أرواحِهم دُفْعَةً واحدة
عِندما يتركونَ شموسَ مَباهِجِهم
في جُفونِ الأَحِبَّة ...
سطوةُ الملحِ تقسو كثيراً
على طائرِ الروحِ إنْ جَاوزَ الشطَّ في نَزقٍ
واستجابَ لسربِ أَمَانٍ
تلوحُ على جَسَدِ الماءِ
في خِفَّةٍ ...

TAKE ME TO MY BODY
*Ali Al Hazmi, Saudi Arabia*


A woman said to the traveler: Take me to the sea,
There, I was born on the passion of the waves
The winds carry me on a journey
Of which I recall nothing but expatriation
Propagating in the wasteland of my soul,
No longer does my need for a little luck
Aid me with more patience
To toss the embers of my long delay


A boy says to a girl tucking her fingers
Under the buttons of his jacket, pouringly
Let my desire in your crowdedness
Float a little on the surface of the water
For the sea is wasting our chance
Of finding refuge in a nostalgic wreath, we weaved
On cheerful nights,
Embrace me longer, for those embraces lull
our singes awaiting the distant,
let my candle in my absence die and light
with the longing of lovers, the dimness of this night,
He knew
The sky would rain again
In the absence of his hands … and he didn't wait!
I fear the sea …
You, like me, fear the sea?!
And it is the flute of nature, the plains of longing,
The refuge of the universe!

I fear the sea for you, the shore eroding under its feet
in all seasons
We will be weary I told you yesterday:
Take me to my body … we repose!
We will be weary if the coasts rain us
With the thirst salient in its silence,
We will be weary, if the distance fences us
In this metallic apathy, the dream became for us
Further than a vine in the hands


Seamen asking about the sea!
How could they retreat to its saltiness?
After all those years!
What is left for them in its waters?
Except for the glistening of seaweeds and the bitter
exhaustion?!


The far lands that faded their strive
Breaking the paddles of their desires
No longer look back
To the fires of their stares whenever they ask
About the wind: What did it want
From directing the helm of their journey towards
languish?
Those going to the sea lose
All the pearls of their souls altogether
When they leave the suns of their joyfulness
In the eyes of their loved ones

The dominance of the salt is being too harsh
On the soul's gull as it passes the shore in petulance
And responds to a safety swarm
Looming on the water's body
Lightly …

## TO TYLKO WIATR
*Alicja Maria Kuberska, Polska*

Wiatr płynie przeciągłą melodią wśród drzew,
dźwięcznie szeleści akordami liści,
rozprasza cienie przelatujących ptaków,
przegania stada kłębiastych chmur,
układa ruchome kolaże na niebie.

Podmuchem zmarszczył taflę jeziora,
ukradł wodzie gładkie oblicze.
Namalował szarością szerokie kręgi,
strząsnął kilka suchych gałązek,
zaświstał na wierzbowej fujarce.

Gdzieś w oddali wtóruje mu echo,
śpiewa w kanonie z kroplami deszczu,
powtarza refren piosenki
i woła mnie – Tęsknię za tobą.
Gdzie jesteś kochanie?

# IT IS JUST WIND
*Alicja Maria Kuberska, Poland*

Wind flows like a long melody among the trees
and rustles resonantly with the chords of leaves,
scatters the shadows of flying birds,
arranges moving collages in the sky
 and chases a herd of clouds.

It rippled the surface of the lake with a gust
and stole the smooth face from the water.
Later, it painted wide circles in grayness,
shook off a few dry twigs
and played a tune with a willow pipe.

Somewhere in the distance, it echoes
sings in a canon with rain drops
—repeats the chorus of the song.
And it calls me, "I miss you.
Where are you, my darling?"

UNTERM SEGEL
*Anna Würth, Deutschland*

Seliges Segeln
aber wehe
wenn unerwartet der Wind dreht
jäh das Boot kippt
das dich begräbt

wenn du untergehst
und versuchst hastig aufzusteigen
wenn du dich emporkämpfst
und auf einen Widerstand triffst

das große schwere Leinensegel
nicht beiseite schieben kannst
und stößt und stößt
vergeblich

wenn dich die Kraft verlässt
dir die Luft ausgeht
du nicht mehr atmen kannst
die Hoffnung weicht
das Wasser zum Gefängnis wird
zum Sargdeckel das Segel
dann zieht die Nacht auf
dann krallt dich
Todesangst
die du nie mehr vergisst
die dir in den Leib geschrieben wird
und bleibt

und wenn du dann
in allerletzter Sekunde
von kundiger Hand gerettet wirst
wenn du hinaufgezogen
wirst aus dem Grab
ins Leben
wird auch das dir
in den Leib geschrieben
für immer

# UNDER THE SAIL
*Anna Würth, Germany*
*Translated by John Waterfield, UK*

Blissful sailing
but beware
when the wind shifts suddenly
sharply tilts the boat
that buries you

when you go under
and try to rise hastily
when you struggle up
and meet resistance

the big heavy canvas sail
you cannot push aside
you push and push
in vain

when your strength leaves you
the air goes from your lungs
you cannot breathe
hope ebbs
the water becomes a prison
the sail a coffin lid
then night falls
then you are clutched
by fear of death
that you never forget
that is written in your body
and remains

and when you then
in the nick of time
are rescued by expert hands
when you are pulled up
out of the grave
into life
this too will be
written in your body
forever

# DOS SONETOS PERSUADIDOS
# POR EL VIENTO: REMOLINOS

*Annabel Villar, Uruguay/España*

La mañana se tiñe en su vaivén
con grises nubarrones que en el cielo
se adueñan del espacio con desvelo
y el viento barre el suelo con desdén.

Hojas de otoño con ocre pereza,
despiertan y escuchan los sones del aire,
se arremolinan con viejo donaire
llenando el ambiente de añeja tibieza.

Pero al final del baile triunfa el viento,
sumiéndolas en vértigos de torbellino,
y ya no pueden danzar a su aliento.

Se elevan sin concierto en un momento,
girando en espiral de remolino
y caen a la tierra como un lamento.

El viento es un espectro que se esfuma
sin un rastro ni una señal detrás
y sin embargo, su presencia suma
una esencia a la vida que no es fugaz.

Desde el tierno soplo primaveral
que bisbisea entre árboles y ramas
hasta el más feroz huracán invernal
que desgarra las nubes con su llama.

Es el viento un emblema de la vida
la fuerza que en el mundo se desliza
y sin embargo no tiene medida.

Así, el viento nos muestra su grandeza
aunque disimule siendo una brisa
y al soplar nos lleva hacia esa certeza.

TWO SONNETS PERSUADED
BY THE WIND: SWIRLS
*Annabel Villar, Uruguay/Spain*
*Translated by Janine Troutman, Germany*

The morning is dyed in its swing
with gray clouds that in the sky
take over the space with carelessness
and the wind sweeps the ground with disdain.

Autumn leaves with ocher laziness,
wake up and listen to the sounds of the air,
they swirl with old grace
filling the atmosphere with vintage warmth.

But at the end of the dance, the wind triumphs,
plunging them into whirlwind vertigos,
and they can no longer dance to their breath.

They rise without a concert in a moment,
Spinning, swirling spiral,
and falling to the ground like a lament.

The wind is a phantom that vanishes
leaving no trace, no sign behind
and yet, its presence adds
an essence to life that is not fleeting.

From the tender breath of spring
that whispers between trees and branches
even the fiercest winter hurricane
that tears the clouds with its flame.

The wind is an emblem of life
the force that into the world slides
and yet it has no measure.

Thus, the wind shows us its greatness
though it disguises itself as a breeze
and when it blows, it takes us towards that certainty.

# HAARE IM WIND
*Antje Stehn, Deutschland*


Man sollte den kleinen Bereich zwischen
dem eigenen Leben
und der Gesellschaft
nicht unterschätzen
an dieser Schwelle ballen sich
Konflikte und Blut
auf Schwellen kämpfen Menschen für Freiheit
Frauen legen ihre Haare in den Wind
verbrennen ihre Schleier
trotzen Schlagstöcken und Gewehrkugeln
für ein menschenwürdiges Leben
ohne Geschlechterapartheid.
Mit wehenden Haaren
schauen wir von den Schwellen
auf unsere Gärten
lange vor der Aussaat der Religion angelegt
bevor Männer und ihre heiligen Bücher
die Gesetze diktierten
unsere Gärten waren für Kletterpflanzen
mit tastendem Denken gedacht
die ihre Ranken hin zum Gegenüber schlingen
zum Nachbarn
zum Dorf
zur Menschheit
Gärten
für das Zusammensein.

# HAIR IN THE WIND
*Antje Stehn, Germany*
*Translated by Betty Gilmore, USA*

Never underestimate
the tiny space between private and public
that threshold
where conflict concentrates itself
the threshold
where voices shout out for freedom
where women let their hair
blow freely in the wind
burn their veils
challenge batons and bullets
fighting to gain their dignity
to gain a life without gender apartheid.
With flowing hair
we stand at the thresholds
and look out at our gardens
growing here long before us
long before the seeds of religion
long before men wrote their holy books
and their laws,
separating women from men
separating men from themselves
the garden was designed for
tentacular climbers
who spread out their arms toward the neighbors
the village
toward humanity
the garden was designed for
togetherness.

## ΑΝΕΜΟΣ ΤΟ ΦΥΣΑ

*Αριστέα Παπαλεξάνδρου, Ελλάδα*

Αυτός ο άνθρωπος
στα θολά ανεβαίνει
μια γυάλινη σκάλα
Κρατά μαύρο περίστροφο
πυρπολεί στον αέρα
εκβιάζει τα σύννεφα
να χιονίσει
Δεν τον βλέπεις συνήθως
με μάτι γυμνό
Τον σκαρώνουν τα άρρωστα
μάτια μυώπων
Οπτασία θα πεις
στο κενό των ανέμων

Και μετά … Να τος σάρκινος
καθιστός σε συμβούλια
Ημερήσια Διάταξη
και είσαι μέσα κι εσύ
σωτηρίας παράδειγμα
Σε καλεί να ανέβεις τη σκάλα
Τρέμεις … άνεμος σε φυσά
Μα επιμένεις

Κι όταν πας να πατήσεις
το πρώτο σκαλί επανέρχεσαι
Δέκα δέκατα όραση
κι ένα βήμα γκρεμός
η αλήθεια
μπροστά σου

# WIND IS BLOWING
*Aristea Papalexandrou, Greece*
*Translated by Philip Ramp, USA/Greece*

This man
is climbing a glass
stairway in mist
He's holding a black revolver
shooting into the air
forcing the clouds
to snow
You ordinarily can't see him
with the naked eye
Eyes suffering from myopia
concoct him
An apparition you'd say
in the winds' void

And then … There he is in the flesh
sitting in committees
The Day's Agenda
and you're there as well
example of redemption
He invites you to climb the stairs
you're trembling … wind blowing on you
But you persist

And just as you're set to step
you're back at the first rung
10/10 vision
the abyss but a stride away
the truth
before you

WATER SIGN
*Ayeshah Émon, Planet Earth*

Sometimes
the thick black blankets of Irish clouds make me
forget
that there are stars beyond
that there is still a sun
that there is no wind on the moon
sometimes
when the pelting rain calls upon my tears to flow
as endlessly as itself
it, too, is seeking a friend
the warmth of my native land is now
as distant to me as the Irish sun
I miss my fire
I have too much water
and now I must make friends with the rain

# MY HAIR NO LONGER BLOWS IN THE WIND
*Ayeshah Émon, Planet Earth*

I hide my hair
in a cloak of red and auburn
shades of violet squeezed from a tube
mixed together in a plastic bowl
my unruly curls smothered with enough ammonia
to make a kitchen sink sparkle
once I muzzled this mass of black frizz in a purple
headscarf
my youthful wisps flattened by embroidered lace on
polyester
and matching pink lipstick
teenage modesty could be fashionable
mine walked a tightrope between screaming at the
world
and desiring its acceptance


My bound hair was a veiled strategy hiding an
unbounded sexuality
yearning to know freely
to be limitless in possibility
to explore the edges of creativity
to be known for more than the size of its childbearing
hips
and breastfeeding bosom
a guise of obedience
so that in exchange I could stall my parents for time
to finish school

to convince fanciful suitors and prospective mothers-
in-law
that I was willing fodder for arranged matrimonials
while I was busy making other plans


I came to America
I cut off my hair
I desired to shed from my follicles
generations of shame damning my female line
to drown in a sea of shampoo
voices of morality policing good and evil
on my freshly laundered scalp
I bleached my brownness
queerness
working-class-wanting-to-be-upper-class-ness
I waxed
threaded
cropped
braided any lustrous locks that betrayed carefully
coiffed feminine wiles
My hair protested:
clumps of tiny curls rampaged my morning sheets
I grieved
I wept
I slathered on coconut oil
swallowed vitamins
vacuumed my pillows
it grew back though lighter
my heart refused to grow heavier

my hair no longer blows in the wind
just forever kindles the raging

# WISHING IN THE WIND
*Barry Stevenson, UK/Germany*


I


And tarry not—
what sees thine eye in this:
in this what see the lacing boughs—
thy passing thoughts
in wandering the winter wind?
They owe and diamond, gape and change
at this sad state of things.
O winter wind, my winter wind,
thy windowed mind
awandering,
that finds no end to this,
no end to this,
my wanderer, now tarry not,
and come.

## II

I am the bent branch flocked in snow,
my wanderer; now stare not so—
what sees thine eye but mortal things?
and they must fade and fall
and fall
in this sad state of things
as doth the wind, the winter wind
awandering
that finds no rest nor end to this,
no end to this,
a wanderer—my wanderer,
my wintering, my wanderer,
fall now. I beg thee
come.

WIND GODDESS
*Betty Gilmore, USA*

There it comes again
it takes me by surprise
With that soft warm breath
Like a lover's caress
That slowly drifts away
Then returns
without warning again
With a cold angry gust
That turns the world upside down
while I run and hide
and try to escape
Until at last it calms down

I barely notice its absence
Until it shows up again
And sweeps me up in a playful
embrace
that makes me feel like spring

And just for a while
I long to be wild
And send whispers and howls
through quiet complacent streets
I long to be wild
Like the goddess Oya[*]
And come and go as I please.


[*] Oya—Yoruban goddess of the wind.

# SHIREEN
*Betty Gilmore, USA*

for Shireen Abu Akleh

like the women in Afghanistan
who suffer under the Taliban
you have to hide your hair In Iran

in France
if you cover your hair with a veil
you may get a fine
or go to jail.

My hair is too curly
to blow in the wind
but I remember you Shireen

your soft hair blowing free
your voice like a fresh breeze scattering truth
like lively leaves
set free from unshakable trees

And when I see hair
blowing in the wind
I remember you Shireen
in the rising wind of voices
that cannot be silenced
until we are free again.

## ALL THE WIND'S UNFINISHED KISSES
*Bill Wolak, USA*

To please your open thighs,
my fingers mingle
the patience of stone
with the readiness of light.

Gathered in your embrace,
all the wind's unfinished kisses
excite your flesh through my lips.

Anywhere you're naked,
darkness tosses
a hyacinth into the fire,
and my tongue becomes
a feather riding
the crest of a wave
all the way to the shore.

WIND-SEEKING SEEDS
*Bill Wolak, USA*

Sometimes a key
breaks in the lock,
unexpectedly life vanishes
quicker than the shadow of lightning.
Wherever desire guides your lips,
enjoy the moistening of arousal
in the restless pink
of an opening embrace,
or the grace of the body
bending for pleasure
like ferns climbing daylight.
This flesh was lent to you
with only one command:
open a heart.
Love has the best verbs,
so grind harder against the avalanche
with all the wind's untamable longing.
Your touch spreads the fever
of a wildflower's perfume.
Your kisses are wind-seeking seeds
that risk everything
for their blossoming.

ΕΡΩΤΑΣ
*Χλόη Κουτσουμπέλη, Ελλάδα*

Αν είμαι αέρας, θα γίνω άνεμος,
Αν είμαι Μαΐστρος, θα γίνω Τραμουντάνα.
Αν είμαι ο Φεν των Άλπεων,
ο Μιστράλ της Γαλλίας,
ο Σιμούν της Αραβίας,
αν μπορώ να ξεριζώνω δέντρα
να στριφογυρίζω καμήλες
ή απλώς να σου χαϊδεύω τρυφερά το πρόσωπο,
θα έρθω για σένα.
Μπορεί να σκουπίζεις το πάτωμα
με την ηλεκτρική σου χελώνα,
να πλέκεις κοτσίδες τα μαλλιά μπροστά στον
καθρέφτη,
να καθαρίζεις τα τζάμια του γυάλινου κλουβιού σου,
εγώ θα έρθω για σένα.
Ακόμα και αν με αρνηθείς,
θα πετάξεις μαζί μου.
Γιατί στον έρωτα και στον θάνατο
δεν υπάρχει στους θνητούς επιλογή.

LOVE
*Chloe Koutsoumpeli, Greece*

If I were air, I would become wind.
If I were Maistros, I would become Tramountana.
If I am Fen of the Alpes,
Mistral of France,
Simoon of Arabia,
if I can uproot trees
or make camels spin around
or just touch your face tenderly,
I will come for you.
You may be sweeping the floor
with your electric turtle,
you may be braiding your hair in front of your mirror
you may be cleaning the glass walls of your cage
I will come for you.
Even if you deny me,
you will fly with me.
Mortals have no choice
in matters of love or death.

# QUALUNQUE NOME GLI DARAI
*Claudia Piccinno, Italia*

Sibila, soffia, serpeggia
Tra verdi chiome
E azzurri infissi.
Plana su bianche terrazze
Scompigliando il bucato.
Solleva le gonne delle donne.
Si posa leggero
dopo la pioggerellina di marzo.
Parte da terra o da mare.
Cambia nome e potenza.
Si misura in nodi
E ingarbuglia pensieri.
Alimenta le fiamme
Semina cambiamento
Sfinito si accascia
Senza preavviso.

Folate, mulinelli, brezza,
vortici, spirali,
tsunami, uragani,
son solo alcuni nomi comuni.
Bora, Maestrale, Scirocco, Libeccio
Nomi propri da codificare.
Comunque lo si chiami
Sa essere ambivalente.
Distrugge e crea

Rinnova ciò che sfiora
Perché sia semenza
Sparsa a caso
In attesa di sbocciare.

# WHATEVER NAME YOU GIVE IT
*Claudia Piccinno, Italy*

It hisses, it blows, it snakes
Among green foliage
And blue window frames.
It glides over white terraces
Messing the laundry.
It lifts women's skirts.
It settles lightly
after the March drizzle.
It departs from land or sea.
It changes name and power.
It is measured in knots
And tangles thoughts.
It feeds the flames
Sows change
Exhausted, he collapses
Without notice.


Gusts, eddies, breeze,
blasts, spirals,
tsunamis, hurricanes
are just a few common names.
Bora, Mistral, Sirocco, Libeccio
Proper nouns to encode it.
Whatever you call it
it can be ambivalent.
It destroys and creates

Renewing what it touches
Because it's seed
Randomly scattered
Waiting to blossom.

# LOS SONIDOS INAUDIBLES
*Daniel Calabrese, Argentina*


Dejamos andar el micrófono
toda la noche en un bosque desolado.

Al otro día hicimos correr la grabación
pero no se oyó más que un soplido.
Era como el viento metálico
de un planeta estéril.

La hicimos correr más rápido.
Aparecieron entonces los ruidos bajos
como si una conversación entre dos árboles
se expandiera desde el campo
hacia la Ruta Dos.

La hicimos correr más rápido aún
y los sonidos crecieron
como la conversación de dos árboles que crecen
y que si uno escucha bien,
con la cabeza apoyada en la madera,
en algún momento parecen crujir
palabras como "espejo", "espejismo",
y muy lentamente palabras como
"cruces", "crucetas",
"humilladero".

THE SOUNDLESS SONGS
*Daniel Calabrese, Argentina*
*Translated by Katherine M. Hedeen, Argentina*


We left the microphone going
all night in an abandoned forest.

The next day we played back the recording
but couldn't hear anything but a whoosh.
It was like the metallic wind
of a sterile planet.

We played it back faster.
Then low noises began to emerge
like a conversation between two trees
spreading out over the country
toward Route 2.

We played it back even faster
and the sounds swelled
like the conversation between two trees growing
and if you listen close
with your head up against the wood
at some point it seems like the creaking
of words like "mirror," "mirage,"
and then words so slowly like
"rood," "crossbeam,"
"wayside cross."

ΓΟΡΔΙΟΣ ΔΕΣΜΟΣ
*Δημήτρης Π. Κρανιώτης, Ελλάδα*

Θέλω να νιώθω
Το καθετί ακούω
Να πω
Το καθετί αγγίζω
Και η αναπνοή
Που σβήνει
Να γίνει αετός

Θέλω να γίνω
Άνεμος
Να λύσω
Τον Γόρδιο δεσμό
Του τέλους και του ύπνου
Να λύσω
Να θρηνήσω
Να παίξω
Ν' αγαπήσω

# GORDIAN KNOT
*Dimitris P. Kraniotis, Greece*

I want to feel
Everything I hear
To say
Everything I touch
And the breath
That fades away
To become an eagle

I want to become
Wind
To untie
The Gordian Knot
Of the end and of sleep
To solve
To mourn
To play
And to love

# ROAD RAGE
*Don Krieger, USA*

I passed on the right, then switched and sprinted by two more. He cut in front, his brake lights coming at me with a gut sick startle. I opened the phone to call the cops, then wished instead for a brick, a glass bottle, a full doggy bag, a shotgun. Before I could write his plate number, he switched lanes and raced away off the exit like the fleeting edge of an eclipse. I shrank, trembling from the grip of it, then sped forward in traffic.

# EIGHTH GRADE SHOP
*Don Krieger, USA*

I planed and glued a large birch blank, turned it down
to a lamp with flared base, fluted body, formed neck
and throat, three-way socket, matching shade, sanded
glass smooth and varnished, all blond like Mom's hair.
Then I made another, same shape and hardware for
Mildred, who came once a month, washed the walls
and bathroom, who told me years later that her teen
son was thrown from a speeding car and killed. I
made that second lamp for Mildred, the curves,
balance and finish finer, and under the varnish colored
with a maple stain.

# FĂȚARNICII
*Dorel Cosma, Romania*

E plină lumea
de fățarnici,
de soi rău,
înveninat
și am crezut
că pot ,
cu voi,
să trecem,
să-i aducem
la liman.
E plină lumea
de fățarnici,
de ipocriți
jucați de actori
în vechea Grecie,
iar astăzi
să îi vezi pe stradă,
când,
cu cortina trasă,
continuă
să-și joace
rolul de fățarnici.
„Cunoaște-te pe tine însuți!”
le-ar fi strigat
de-atunci-Socrate
sperând să fie potabilă
licoarea otrăvită.
Dar vântul

i-a oprit ideea
şi a zburat făţărnicia
cu ură şi furie
în miez de lume caldă.
Şi i-am primit cu braţele deschise
în lumea plină de culori,
crezând
că vom opri furtuna
prin simţ şi suflet de valori.
Precum nici Platon,
Metodiu, Chiril
sau Tesla
n-au reuşit a vindeca
duhoarea ipocriziei,
nici lumea caldă
şi plină de culori
nu a putut
să stingă
vârtejul urii,
din seaca inimă
de ipocriţi uneltitori.
E plină lumea
de făţarnici,
de falsul
sufletului infectat,
de vântul puterii
ascuns sub masca
de ratat.
Dar,
chiar francezii,

prin Dumas
ne-nvață,
că masca
chiar de-i bine regizată
„cu doar puțină atenție
o deosebim de față".
E plină lumea
de fățarnici.
Și noi, cei mulți,
cu farmecul culorii,
Noi,
i-am primit
în Casa Artei
cu muzică și dans
și le-am crezut
cuvântul veninos.
Nici chiar atunci
când violența,
prin forța pumnului
dezlănțuit în masă,
nu am crezut
ca răul să domine,
și le-am deschis
din nou,
portița omeniei.
Dar,
lumea e plină
de fățarnici
ce se tărăsc prin viață,
iar Universul

a obosit el însuşi.
Şi-atunci,
ce facem noi
cu şleahta
de furioşi, războinici,
ce vor să rupă
a minţii nobilime?
Să-i arătăm cu degetul
chiar şi atunci când tac,
ca lumea să-i cunoască
şi-aceşti demenţi făţarnici
să zboare dintre noi.

# THE HYPOCRITES
*Dorel Cosma, Romania*

The world is full
of hypocrites,
a bad kind
poisoned
and I thought
that we could
together,
move them,
and make both
ends meet.
The world is full
of hypocrites,
of hypocrites
played by actors
in ancient Greece,
while today
we see them on the street
When,
with the curtain drawn,
they keep going
always playing
the role of hypocrites.
"Know yourself!"
one would have shouted at them
since-Socrates
hoping they would swallow
poisoned liquor.
But the wind

stopped the idea
and hypocrisy flew away
with hatred and anger
in the middle of a warm world.
And we welcome them with open arms
in the colorful world
thinking
that we will stop the storm
by sense and a set of values.
Like Plato,
Methodius, Cyril
or Tesla
they failed to heal
the stench of hypocrisy
nor the warm world
both full of colors
could not
to extinguish
this maelstrom of hate
from the bottom of the heart
of scheming hypocrites.
The world is full
of hypocrites,
with fake
the infected souls,
with the wind, the power
hidden under the mask
about to be missed.
But,
even the French

referring to Dumas
teach us
that a mask
even if it is well-directed
"with just a little care
we distinguish it from the beginning".
The world is full
of hypocrites.
And we, the many,
with the charm of color,
We,
welcome them
in the House of Art
with music and dance
and I believed their
poisonous word.
Not even then
when violence,
the force of the fist
unleashed en masse,
I didn't believe
for evil to rule,
and I opened up to them
again,
the gate of humanity.
But,
the world is full
of hypocrites
that creep through life,
and the universe

is itself tired.
And then,
what do we do
with the sleight
of angry warriors,
what do they want to break
in noble minds?
Let's point our finger at them
even when I'm silent
for the world to know
these demented hypocrites
and make them go away.

## SÖZÜN BEDENSİZ EVİ
*Elçin Sevgi Suçin, Türkiye*

saçları beyaz değil
fakat hatırlıyor dünyanın ilk günlerini
kokusunu ve korkusunu âdem'in
havva'nın toprağa gömdüğü ilk çekirdeği

sözün bedensiz evi
toplayıp bütün çığlıkları genişliyor an be an
ve gürültülü bir gezegene dönüşüyor
döndükçe çoğaltıyor sesleri

bu gece eski bir mektubu okuyor
sözün bakırıyla yazılmış taş yapraklara
ilk isyandan bahsediyor lilith'den
ve çocuklarından onun:
kölelik ve cennet aynı cümlede

ilk uyanan kurtulur
ilk işiten rüzgârın söylediklerini
rüzgâr ki suyun toprağın havanın
bilmediklerini bilir ve ateşe yön verir
nefesin gücüyle

mevsimlerin hermes'i
bu sabah lir çalıyordu yapraklar dökülürken
ve vakti giydiriyordu bir sarı bir yeşil
yakamda bir dal yıldız çiçeği
kulak kesildim fısıldayıp durduklarına

# FLESHLESS HOUSE OF WORD
*Elçin Sevgi Suçin, Turkey*

It has no gray hair,
Yet it remembers the early days of Earth,
The fragrance and fear of Adam,
The first seed Eve buried in the soil.

The fleshless house of word
Collects all cries at all times, expanding,
And turns into a noisy planet,
Amplifying voices as it turns around.

Tonight, it reads an old letter,
Committed to stone leaves with the copper of word,
Talking of the first mutiny of Lilith
And her children:
Bondage and Elysium in the same sentence.

Delivered will be the one who awakens first,
The one who first heeds what the wind tells,
The wind knows what the soil and the air
Know not, and steers the flame,
With the force of breath.

Hermes of seasons
Was playing lyre this morning as leaves came down,
And she clothed time with yellow, then green.
A bough of dahlia on my collar,
I was all ears to what it whispered on.

# RÜZGÂR BENİMLE
*Emel Koşar, Türkiye*

şehre yayılan köpüklerinde
yanık reçel kokusu
keder bir taş gibi içimde saklı
hayal halkaları
çiçeğe dönüşen tohum
yıllar yağdı saçlarıma
yakaladığım iklimde
enkaza dönüşmüş tedirginliğim
rüyalarını gönder bana
kaderin boğazından
erimiş altın döktürdüm
kayboldum Morpheus'un rüyasında
dertlerimi kuşandım geldim
gücümün gölgesinden kork
depremin sağanağından
sadece külü tattım, yağmuru bekledim
güneş gülüşünde
kristal saklı bakışlarım

# THE WIND IS WITH ME
*Emel Koşar, Turkey*
*Translated by Yaprak Damla Yıldırım, Turkey*

spreading across the city
your foam smells like burnt jams
sorrow lurks in me like a stone
circles of fantasy
the seed which turned into a flower
years rained down on my hair
my uneasiness which turned into a wreck
in the climate i embraced
send me your dreams
i had the melted gold poured
down the throat of destiny
and got lost in the dream of Morpheus
girded my troubles on here i am
beware of the shadow of my power
of earthquake downpours
i tasted ash alone and waited for the rain
my crystal looks
are at your laugh made of sun

# STRANI VJETAR

*Emina Čabaravdić-Kamber, Njemačka/Bosna i Hercegovina*

Ponekad pušemo zajedno u ritmu
ljuljamo se u zraku tamo i amo
ne nalazimo mjesto
niti dodir sa zemljom
gdje bi se sretni ugnijezditi mogli

Ponekad nismo u sklopu
gura me sa sjevera prema jugu
sklon je da se vidi kao spasitelj
u kamenitoj zemlji mog siromašnog bića

Ponekad djeluje kao izgubljeni vjetar
Koji na klisurama
Malo koje stablo formira
umoran od puta tamo i amo
veže me kao čvrstu žilu za tuđe tlo

WIND-DRIVEN
*Emina Čabaravdić-Kamber, Germany/Bosnia Herzegovina*
*Translated from German by Gino Leineweber, Germany/Italy*

Sometimes, we blow as it were
Sway back and forth in the air
Find no place
No relation to earth
To snuggle in happily

Sometimes, we are not in harmony.
He shoos me from the north to the south
Inclined to be seen as a hero
In the stony homeland
Of my barren existence

Sometimes, the wind, which forms
Few trees on cliffs confuse me
When tired of immortal to and fro
Holds me with solid roots
On foreign ground

# FORTUNE IS THE WIND
*George Wallace, USA*

Fortune is casual betrayal writ in large letters and in small; it is crime and punishment, it is truth scrawled on ghetto walls, lies covered in the irreducible fur of appetite;

Fortune comes in small packages; the form of an ulcer on the lip, or the jaundice you spit back into a cup; it is pronounced by the gods, not men, it is carried for secret generations;

In the blood, in the semen; in the bad habit of talking out of turn or being bitten on the ankle by a snake;

Or plagued with club foot;

Fortune is also misfortune, it comes with a kicker; good luck is getting away with it, bad luck is your mother coughing up blood at the dinner table;

And worse luck is having a neighbor with an
incurable grievance concerning men with beards;

And worse luck yet is the cop who pulls you over and
has a twitch in his trigger finger bigger than the
Fourth of July;

Vengeance is a cheat, and premeditated kindnesses
will come back to haunt you; therefore, take good
luck with the bad; kidney failure, blackouts, brown
tide in your bones;

Stock market futures, fortune tellers with their hands
out; grandfathers who go mad as money in upstairs
rooms; grandmothers in kitchens, painting images of
christ or the devil and decorating Easter eggs;

Fortune is a drug, it has all the right moves, it waits
until it is the right time to act and then it kicks down
your door and does its dirty work; fortune is the
unplanned slip of a surgeon's knife; fortune is waiting
for you in the hotel lobby with a message from hell;

Fortune is a toilet that backs up, a wound that won't
heal, it is a misstep committed in the fog of war or
lovemaking, swallowed up and forgotten; twenty
years later it returns in your soup;

Fortune is a stranger with a broken tooth who wants to
fuck you up with a knife for play, and leave you for
dead on the commuter train;

And a roof collapses, and a child of 20 refuses to look
you in the eye,

This is the way of the world; the world goes hysterical
at your touch; it hurls insults and unfair accusations at
the dinner table, it throws plates; it curses god in the
emergency room;
It purples gums; the world worries your fists and
seduces you with rumors and lies;

Meanwhile, fortune takes it all in, calmly; fortune is
incomplete sentences, fortune is the helpless hunger
that eats its way through your heart;

Fortune is blind, fortune is the wind—
fortune is waiting for you in the idiot dark;

You end your days as you began them, in doubt or
shock or disbelief, carrying unmentionable grievances
to your grave;

Cross your fingers, spit for luck.

# DAS IST DER WIND
*Gino Leineweber, Deutschland/Italien*


Der Wind der das Segel bläht
Dich hoch über das Wasser schießt
Das ist der Wind

Der Wind der brüllend die Wogen aufpeitscht
Mit jedem Schlag Regen Pfeile versprüht
Das ist der Wind

Der Wind der in der Höhe Sturmwolken jagt
Am Boden keine Blätter und Blüten lässt
Das ist der Wind

Der Wind der meiner Liebsten Stimme verleiht
Mich tobend in ihre sehnenden Arme treibt
Das ist der Wind

# THAT IS THE WIND
*Gino Leineweber, Germany/ Italy*
*Translated by Barry Stevenson, UK/Germany*

The wind that billows out the sail
Shoos you up and over the water
That is the wind

The roaring wind whips up the waves
With each blow spits arrows of rain
That is the wind

The wind that chases stormclouds high
Spares no leaves or blooms below
That is the wind

The wind that lends my darling voice
Drives me raging to her yearning arms
That is the wind

THE WIND
*Hussein Habasch, Kurdistan*


I close the door,
it comes from the window.
I close the window,
it comes from under the door.
I close under the door,
it comes from the window slit.
I close the window slit,
it comes from the chimney.
I close the chimney hole,
it comes from the keyhole.
I close the keyhole,
it comes from a place I do not know!
This wind does not let me breathe anything else,
and I don't understand the reason for all this love it
has for me!
So, I open the door and windows wide
and let it hug me like an old friend!


MERCY
*Hussein Habasch, Kurdistan*


A bird built his nest
Atop a high tree.
The tree called God
I beg you, God,
Do not send storms in my direction.

# மாற்றத்தின் காற்று
*ஹேமா ரவி, இந்தியா*

பல நேரங்களில் மேல் காற்றோட மெல்ல
நெளிவு-சுளிவுகளைக் கடந்து செல்ல
வேண்டும். புரிந்துக்கொள், நீயொன்றும்
விரைவில்
உருகி அணையப்போகும் மெழுகுவர்த்தி
அல்ல.


புயல் காற்றுப் போல் உள்ள எதிரிகளை
வென்று
சவால்களை எதிர்க்கொண்டு
நகைப்பவர்களை தாண்டிச் சென்று
அவர்களின் துடுப்பை பிடுங்கிவிடு
ஆம்! சூறாவளியின் பொழுது, உனது
நினைவுகளை நங்கூரமிடு
எண்ணங்களில் சுனாமியை
கட்டுப்படித்திடு.

தீயை என்றுமே விசிறி விடாதே
சிதைக்கப்பட்டு, நெளியளுடன் நிற்காதே

வாழ்க்கை ஒரு தென்றல் –
மென்மையான 'செஃபிர்' காற்று,
சூறாவெளி மற்றும் இளவேனிற் காற்று
வீசுகின்றன
நீர்த்துளிகள் ஆறுகளாய் ஓடுகின்றன
மாற்றத்தின் காற்று தெளிவாக உள்ளது –
தென்றலுடன் செல்.

WINDS OF CHANGE
*Hema Ravi, India*

At all times, you need to breeze along
past twists and turns.
Understand that you're not
a flickering candle that'd melt soon.

You can maneuver challenges and move past
gales of laughter, knock-off opponents,
strip them of their sails …
Yes! During hurricanes, remain anchored
with the tsunami of thoughts sublimated.

Never fan the flames
Also, learn not
to be left to twist and squirm.

Life's a breeze—
gentle zephyr,
tornadoes and gusty winds blow,
drops of water flow as rivers.
The winds of change are evident—
Breeze along …

# RÜZGAR GIDIP GELIYORDU ARAMIZDA
*Hilal Karahan, Turkey*

Soyunur rengini gece
gümüş otların üzerinde
sere serpe

Büyür ıslıklar
ıslak fısıltılar
toprak büyür

Kokulu yağlarla
ovar ılgınları
o eski yazlardan kalma
avare rüzgâr

Gecenin alnı ak
kolları kalın
yumuşak

Gecede
sonsuzdur
atlası tenin

# THE WIND WAS SHUTTLING BETWEEN US
*Hilal Karahan, Turkey*

The night takes its color off
and carelessly spreads
over the silver grass

The whistles grow,
wet are the whispers
and grows the earth

A vagabond wind
—a residue of ancient summers—
climbers the tamarisks
with scented oils

Blameless is the night
thick and soft
are her arms

The night makes
eternal
the flesh's atlas

TREOW, THE EQUIVALENCE
OF TREE AND TRUTH
*Holly Iglesias, USA*


I take as my sermon's text the lowest limbs of the
oldest oak in Audubon Park, my lesson one of
grandmothers who died on elm-lined streets one after
the other, of a soft wind blowing through a stand of
cottonwoods that sighed for love of them, and then, as
recessional, a litany of the weeds of the Midwest to
help us forget that scorching summer, that poplar
felled by a tornado, that hard winter with no toys
under the Christmas tree, that day I peeked through an
iron gate at frangipani and wondered, Where am I?




Once, the idea of Kansas filled a book and then a
movie that opened onto a windbreak of river birch, a
farmhouse on a hill, a swarm of insects, the husband
away somewhere, and a shift in the wind that rattled
the storm shutters, set the sashes to whispering while
sheets flapped on a line near the sickle pear that was
once the woman's delight.

In the last century, a Pygmy was displayed among
geisha girls and Navajo weavers at a World's Fair full
of artificial light and faux thatched huts. His captor,
hearing of his death years later, prayed that the little
man had come to rest back home in the Congo
beneath trees he knew as God when, in fact, he died in
a tobacco barn in Virginia by his own hand. Today, a
shoeless man lies napping under the canopy of a tulip
tree, the breeze loosing petals to blanket his sleep, for
it is springtime, springtime, springtime in the
heartland.

WIND
*Janine Troutman, Germany*

Blustering, buffeting Wind swelled to a
crescendo
as it set about the old farmstead.

Casement windows flew open.
Dislodged tiles slid loose
to lie in fragments on the
debris scattered ground.
In a lost corner, a forlorn spider
clung to her swaying web.

But it is not Wind,
but the workings of Wind,
that whistle and whisper
that creak and clang
that rustle and rush
that blast and bang
that whine and whimper
that crack and crash

Call in the grubby, boisterous children.
Fetch in the frantically flapping sheets.
Tie the tarpaulins tight over the wood pile.
Close the shutters, fasten the latches,
Bolt the door.

Let flustered Mother, hair all awry,
gather her scattered thoughts,
fold away the clean linen,
draw around her shawl.
Let work weary Father,
put the kettle on the hob,
light the fire in the hearth,
rearranging twigs and logs.

And let inhaling Wind draw the smoke
up and out of the puffing chimney pots.

Now, Wind is no longer odorless,
as he fills the air with his acrid breath.
Now, he is no longer naked and trembling,
but dressed and dancing,
lightly shrouded in whisps and whirls,
spiraling into columns of shimmering grey.

Inside, in a high-up corner,
a spider diligently spins a new web.

WIND´S OFFERINGS
*Janine Troutman, Germany*

Generous as a genie set free from his uncorked bottle,
The wind is eager to bring you his offerings:
some sweet, some sour, some grotesque, some bizarre,
some enchantingly perfumed, some highly
embarrassing,
not to forget the undeniable witnesses to death and
decomposition.

So, while in the city, toxic fumes snarl from belching
exhausts and
sulfurous stench blasts out from industrial estates;
while acrid smoke spirals from double-breasted
chimneys and
provokes tears, stinging as sliced onion on the
chopping board,
mown lawns refresh parks and suburbs where red-
rose, jasmine-yellow
and dusky-musk scents slowly evaporate from cut
glass flasks on dressing tables.

Though out in the country, fetid emanations steam
from freshly laid dung,
like the wretched foul breath that exits the cavities of
rotting teeth,
on terraced upper slopes, the heady buzz of bee-loved
almond blossom
bee-witches in swirling petals of scattering pink-white
snow.

100

Bells ring out from hilltop temples, and intoxicating aromatic incense
floats down over valleys filled with villages and rice fields.

However, when generous Wind abates to sleep a while,
a work-weary genie retiring self-satisfied to his bottle,
it is Rain´s clear water that washes the slates of the dwellings clean,
that drives all Wind´s offerings deep into the dark earth and
leaves freshly rinsed Air to hang out and dry.

# ӨНГӨРСНӨӨС ИРСЭН САЛХИ

*Жэнни Лхагвасүрэн, Монгол*

Салхи, чи
Өмнөх төрөлд минь
Үс хийсгэж байсан тэр салхи мөн үү
Салхи, чи
Өнгөрсөн амьдралын минь
Саарыг мэдэх тэр салхи мөн үү
Салхи, чи
Үйлдсэн бүхнийг минь харж байсан
Тэр салхи мөн үү
Хайранд би өгөөмөр хандсан болов уу
Хайхрамжгүй эсвэл гишгэчин хаясан болов уу
Үнэн худал хоёрыг ялгаж таньдаг байсан уу
Үнэгэн залинд автан алдаж эндэж явсан уу
Эрх мэдэлтэнд бөхөлзөж
Эд хөрөнгөнд шунамхайран байв уу
Өнгөний хойноос хөөцөлдөж явав уу
Өөдтэй биш гээд хялайж явсан уу
Хэлж өгөөч салхи минь
Үс хийсгэн зөрөөд өнгөрөх салхи чи
Өмнөх олон төрөлд минь байсан тэр салхи мөн үү

# A WIND FROM MY PAST LIFE
*Jenny Lkhagvasuren, Mongolia*

The Wind,
Are you the same wind that blew my hair in my
former existence?
The Wind,
Are you the same wind that knows about my
transgressions from a prior life?
The Wind,
Are you the same wind that saw every choice I made
back then?
The Wind, please tell me,
If I showed deep respect for someone's love
Or if I just ignored it?
Did I have the aptitude to distinguish between truth
and lies?
Did I get lost in the lies and end up not realizing my
ignorance?
Did I flatter the authorities by obtaining power and
wealth?
Did I get blinded by any physical appearance?
The Wind, do you remember
When I would judge people based on their appearance
And disrespect them?
The Wind that blows my hair,
Are you the same wind that was in my previous
incarnations?

DASHURI NË KOHË LUFTE
*Jeton Kelmendi, Kosovë/ Belgjikë*

Nganjëherë dua të ndodhin
Krejt gjërat
Ndryshe
Për shembull, me ra mjegulla e dendur,
Sa të kalohet më lehtë
Kufiri,
Të kalohet atypari
Ku disa muaj më parë
Kam parë një vajzë
Kaçurrele,
Së paku ta shoh me sy
E ta ëndërroj pastaj
Duke bërë dashuri.

Fundja
Luftë është dhe luftës
Nuk i dihet:
Përditë duke e mundur vdekjen
Ngjarje të tilla
Se filani e fisteku
Ranë për liri,
Apo edhe lajme tjera,
Si p.sh. Armikut iu asgjësuan
Kaq e kaq...
Këto pra janë përditshmëri.
Ndoshta
T'i thuash dikujt
Se në kohë lufte dëshiron
Dashuri,
Dikush të merr për të marrë,
Por edhe në më të përgjakshmet

Luftëra,
Ushtari mendjen s'e heq prej dashurisë
Atë kohë vetë e kam parë.

Kohë lufte është
Zoti e di
Si do t'i vijë fundi,
Ndoshta
As kohë s'ka më për dashuri,
Koha e bën të veten
Por, sikur të gjithë të mbjellin
Vdekjen,
Kush do ta korrte
Dashurinë.

Poeti mendon
Se dashuritë më të mëdha
Lindin në kohë luftërash,
Ndoshta,
Ndoshta tejkalojnë përmasat
E një rrëfimi biblik,
Ose
Edhe historitë më fantastike
Të lorkës dhe heminguejit,
Thjesht
Dashuria është një luftë tjetër,
Më e përjetshmja luftë,
Më e gjatë
Se çdo luftë tjetër,
Por armët janë
Tjera:
Zemra, shpirti dhe seksi.

I dola vetes dore
Dhe vajta
Mu te kryepersonazhi.
Luftë është
A po e sheh dita-ditës
Jeta po bëhet më e mërzitshme:
Kështu disi
Më ka rrapllua mendja,
Teksa
Me qejf të madh po bëheshim gati
Për pak dashuri.

Ëndërr apo zhgjëndërr,
As sot
S'jam i sigurt nëse më pyet
Dikush,
Por, një çudi e madhe
Pat ndodhur
99 herë kam mundur të vdes
99-ën.
Pa luftuar,
Si fillon koha e dashurisë
As që merret me mend,
Haj dashuria bre, he lufta.

Natë e vonë
Dhe hëna sikur ka harruar
Të dalë,
Kthehet ushtari, niset
Betejave të reja.

Njëmend është dashuri në kohë lufte,
Lufta vazhdon...
He ushtar ushtari.

# LOVE IN WARTIME
*Jeton Kelmendi, Belgium/Kosovo*

Sometimes, I want them to happen
These things
Differently
For example, a heavy fog fell on me,
And a border was easily
Crossed—
To pass there, first of all,
Where a few months ago
I saw a girl
With curly hair,
Only saw her—
And to dream later on while
Falling in love.
At the end
It is war, and we don't
know the future
Every day, fighting with death
These stories that
Someone or whomever
Fell for freedom
Or other news,
Such as the enemy
Was destroyed,
These are daily routines.
Perhaps
To share with someone
That he desires love
During wartime,

Someone will think you are stupid
But even in the fiercest fights
A soldier will never stop thinking about love
I have seen it in myself.
In times of war
God knows
How the end will come,
Perhaps
No time has space for love—
Time tolls,
But what if everyone planted
Death
Who would harvest
Love?
A poet thinks
that the greatest loves
Are born in wartime.
Perhaps,
Perhaps—exceeding the imagination
From a bible story,
Or
Even the most illustrated stories
Of Lorca and Hemingway.
Simply
Love is another war,
It's an infinite war
Even the longest war
Longer than any other.
But weapons are
Something else:

Heart, Soul, and Sex.
I came for myself
And went
Right to the center of the stage.
There is war.
Are you looking at it day by day?
Life is becoming even more boring:
This is how it started
My mind was confused me,
And with happiness, we were ready
For a little more love.
Is this a dream or an anti-dream;
Not sure if someone will ask,
Today—
But, surprisingly,
It happened.
99 times, I have been able to die
All 99.
Without war,
How can love begin?
It cannot be imagined.
There is love and war.
Late night
The moon has forgotten
To come outside,
A soldier returns, departs
For other front lines,
When there is love during wartime
War continues …
This is a soldier of a soldier.

EL VIENTO
*Julio Pavanetti, Uruguay/España*

Cuando el viento se enfada y silba fuerte,
los árboles se agitan temerosos,
sus hojas y sus ramas se sacuden
preparándose para combatir,
pero nada va a cambiar en sustancia,
la cólera de un día que se enciende
sin límites, con rumbo aún incierto,
se dispondrá a acabar por restaurar
el equilibrio perfecto y sereno.


Cuando el viento enmudece y se detiene,
los árboles comienzan su latido
aprontándose para descansar
bajo el silencio azul de los recuerdos,
pero nada va a cambiar en sustancia,
la belleza encendida de una noche
estrellada y de un cielo despejado,
se dispondrá a expresar el lado oculto
adonde nunca llegan las miradas.


El corazón del viento siempre late
en dos vertientes que se contradicen,
es símbolo de vida y libertad
y también es transporte de los males,
pero nada va a cambiar en sustancia,
el viento, en positivo o en negativo,

es un valor moral, y es la metáfora
de las supersticiones más antiguas,
de remotas creencias, de locura.

WIND
*Julio Pavanetti, Uruguay/Spain*

When the wind gets angry and whistles loudly,
the trees shake fearfully,
their leaves and branches quiver
preparing to fight
but nothing will change in substance,
the anger of a day that ignites without limits,
with direction still uncertain,
will be ready to finish by restoring
the perfect and serene balance.


When the wind abates and stops,
the trees throb as the sap rises
getting ready to rest
under the blue silence of memories,
but nothing will change in substance,
the burning beauty of a starry night
and a clear sky,
will get ready to reveal the hidden side
that eyes never reach.


The heart of the wind always beats
in two aspects that contradict each other,
It is a symbol of life and freedom.
and it is also a transport of evils,
but nothing will change in substance,
the wind, positive or negative,

is a moral value, and it is a metaphor
of the oldest superstitions,
remote beliefs and madness.

## NACHTHAUCH
*Kirsten Döbler, Deutschland*

Im Andenken<br>an Frank Behrendt

Die Tage sind aus Wind gewebt
frische Brisen schmücken
die Welt im Schutz des Lichts
bunte Bänder umgarnen dich
kitzeln deine Wangen
du wagst dich aus der Deckung

Der Abend knotet leise Litzen
zwingt die Fäden an ihren Platz
im Gehörgang rhythmisch
der Lauf des Webschützens
du spinnst dich ein

Still kommt die Nacht
schneidet deinen Kokon auf
ihr kalter Hauch ritzt dir
eine welke Blüte auf die Stirn

# THE BREATH OF NIGHT
*Kirsten Döbler, Germany*

In Memory<br>of Frank Behrendt

The days are woven from wind
fresh breezes adorn
the world protected by daylight
colored ribbons enchant you
tickle your cheeks
you venture out of hiding

The evening quietly knots heddles
forces the threads into place
lulled by the rhythm
of the weaving shuttle
you swathe yourself in yarn

Silently the night comes
to slit your cocoon
its cold breath carves
a withered bloom on your brow

ΠΡΟΣΚΡΟΥΣΗ
*Λιάνα Σακελλίου, Ελλάδα*

Αχ, μην είστε ανόητες.
Φυσικά μπορείτε ν' αναπνεύσετε.
Ξέρουμε πως λυπάστε.
Μην ανησυχείτε, θα επιστρέψουμε,
ψιθυρίζουν.
Και τσιμουδιά σ' όποιον κι αν έρθει
να σας μιλήσει.
Μα βέβαια, ποιος θα μας μιλούσε
εδώ στο ερημικό νησί;
Για πέστε, με ποιον θα μιλούσαμε;
Οι άντρες έφυγαν,
κατέβηκαν το μονοπάτι
με τις κομμένες φτέρες.
Ήταν αποκαρδιωτικό.
Ούτε ήχος μηχανής. Ούτε πανιά.
Μόνο ο άνεμος από τη θάλασσα.
Χρησιμοποίησαν τα κουπιά.
Ήταν καλά σχεδιασμένο αλλά οι καρδιές μας
έλιωσαν.
Μετά μυρίσαμε τη φωτιά.
Μετά ήρθαν οι ένστολοι στο σπίτι.
Βγήκαμε στις μύτες των ποδιών απ' το υπόγειο,
φορούσαμε τα νυχτικά μας.
Πήραμε μαζί το σκούρο χαλί.
Τι θα μπορούσαμε να κάνουμε;
Πού πάτε βρε κορίτσια;
Πάμε στη θάλασσα.
Τι θα μπορούσαμε να πούμε;

Πάμε να κολυμπήσουμε ενάντια στο ρεύμα.

Γιατί, είστε μάγισσες, κάνετε μάγια;

Αρχίσαμε να γελάμε, να γελάμε σαν να φωνάζουμε.

Αντρέα, τα ρεμάλια μας ξέφυγαν.

Ρε δεν βάσταγες τσίλιες;

Πώς ξέφυγαν;

Ξέφυγαν.

Και εσείς τους βοηθήσατε, κορίτσια.

Όχι, δεν πάτε πουθενά. Θα διασκεδάσουμε εδώ, θα δείτε.

Πολλή πλάκα.

Θα πάμε στη θάλασσα για νυχτερινό μπάνιο, είπαμε κι αρχίσαμε να τρέμουμε.

Φοβόμασταν τα βράχια.

# COLLISION
*Liana Sakelliou, Greece*

Oh, don't be silly,
of course, you can breathe.
I know it's sad.
Don't you worry, we'll be back,
they are whispering.
And don't you go on talking,
no matter who comes here.
Of course not, who would we talk to
out here on the deserted island?
Say, who would talk to us?
The fugitives slipped away
down the path
covered with cut ferns.
How heartbreaking to see them go.
No sound of engines. No sound of sails.
Only the sea wind.
They used oars.
We planned well, but our hearts cracked.
Then we smelled fire.
Then, men in regulation shirts came to our house.
We tiptoed out of the basement in our nightgowns.
Took the dark rug with us.
What could we do?
Where are you going, girls?
We're going to the sea.
What could we say?
We'll swim against the current.
Why, are you pagans or what?

We giggled, giggling like shouting.
Andreas, those sons of bitches got away.
Weren't you on guard?
They got away?
They got away.
And you girls helped them.
No, you are not going anywhere
We'll have fun here, you 'll see. Lots of fun.
We'll go to the sea for a night swim, we replied
and started shaking.
We were afraid of the rocks.

# Ο ΘΡΗΝΟΣ ΤΗΣ ΙΤΑΛΙΔΑΣ ΝΤΙΒΑΣ
*Λίλυ Εξαρχοπούλου, Ελλάδα*

Στην αρχαιότητα οι άνεμοι ήταν Θεοί
Έτσι προσέφεραν στους θνητούς την εύπλοια
Βοηθούσαν κάποιες καλλιέργειες της γης
Αναζωογονούσαν τον αέρα
Κάλυπταν τις δυσοσμίες

Στον Μεσαίωνα πάλι, είχαμε προσευχές
Να συνεχίσουν αμέριμνοι οι Κιχώτες την πορεία τους
Αρκετές ήταν για τον Άι Νικόλα
Προστάτη άγιο των ναυτικών
Για να χηρέψουν λιγότερες μανάδες

Στη νεωτερική εποχή επανεφηύραμε
-πέρα από τις τριήρεις-
τις καραβέλλες -και τις … Ισαβέλλες-
Αντί για ποντοπόρα πλοία
προβάλλαμε Τιτανικούς
υποβρύχια, νάρκες θαλάσσης

Στη μετά- μετανεωτερική εποχή θυμηθήκαμε
Τον έρμο τον Μόμπι Ντικ, τον γέρο και τη θάλασσα,
Την Οδύσσεια μέχρι και «Το παιδί και το δελφίνι»

Χρατς!
Ένα άλμπατρος χάνει το κεφάλι του
Σ' ένα απ΄ τα κοπάδια με τις ανεμογεννήτριες
Κι όλη η ποίηση ησυχάζει!

THE ITALIAN DIVA'S LAMENTATION
*Lily Exarchopoulou, Greece*


In ancient times, the winds were Gods
They offered the mortals a safe sail
Helped in the cultivation of crops
Covered foul, unpleasant smells


In the Middle Ages, Man created prayers
to safeguard the journeys of the lackadaisical
Quixotes
People also appealed to St Nicolas, the marine patron
Urging him to prevent the widowing of mothers


In Modern Times, we had to reinvent
First the triremes, next the caravels—and the …
Isabellas—
Instead of seafaring vessels, we boasted of Titanics,
—rarely yellow—submarines and naval mines


In the meta–Postmodern Age,
We fell in love with *Boy on a Dolphin*
Then we remembered poor *Moby Dick*
As well as *Ulysses* and *The Old Man and the Sea.*


Swoosh!
An albatross loses its head
in the forest of wind turbines
And all poetry is silenced.

# VETAR ZA VREME POMRAČENJA SUNCA NAD PANONIJOM

*Maja Herman Sekulic, Srbija/SAD*

Put preko mosta
Preko reke Save
Preko Dunava
U ravnicu Vojvodine
Na Panonsko more koje
Više ne postoji
Nalik je jedrenju
Po vodama koje su jednom davno
Tu bile
Nalik je otvaranju neba
Ka večnosti
Gde beskrajni usevi žita pune oko
Gde svaki zamah vetra
Izaziva talasanje u okeanu zelenila
U krugovima kukuruza
Kao kamen bačen u vodu
I remeti mrtvu tišinu
Solarne eklipse
U talasu žutog sena
Psst psst kaže talas
Znam ja ovo mesto
Video sam kako plastovi gore na vetru
Koji duva preko senki
Ispod pomračenog sunca
Kao morska oluja koja to nije

# WIND DURING THE SOLAR ECLIPSE
# OVER PANNONIA
*Maja Herman Sekulic, Serbia/USA*

A trip over the bridge
over the Sava River
over the Danube
to flatlands of Vojvodina
to the Pannonian Sea that is
no more
it is like sailing
over the waters that once were
once upon a time—there
it is like opening the sky
to eternity
where endless rows of wheat fill the eye
where each movement of the wind
makes ripples in the ocean green
in circles of corn
like a stone thrown into waters
and disturbs the deaf silence of
the solar eclipse
in the wave of yellow hay
hush hush says the wave
I know this place
I have seen the sun bake those fields
I have seen the haystacks burn in the wind
that blows over shadows
under the darkened sun
like a sea storm that is not

STADTFLUCHT
*Maren Schönfeld, Hamburg*


Hinter grünen Fensterläden verbergen
sich kleine stille Räume
wie ein Wolltuch
das einhüllt

Im sinkenden Abendlicht tanzen
Schatten an der Wand
flackern Kerzen
herzberuhigend

Draußen geht Wind um die Häuser
zaust Laub aus Ästen
wirbelt es über
den Boden

Am Morgen die Fenster öffnen
den Raum mit Kühle
und Klarheit füllen
blaue Luft

Das Tosen der Nacht
aufgelöst in Stille
vor der Tür
bunte Blätter

# FLIGHT FROM THE CITY
*Maren Schönfeld, Germany*
*Translated by Kirsten Döbler, Germany*

Hidden behind green shutters
are small quiet rooms
enfolding me like
a woolen shawl

In the fading evening light
shadows are dancing on the wall
candles flickering
heart-soothing

Outside, the wind blows around corners
ruffling leaves from branches
swirling them across
the ground

In the morning, I open the windows
to fill the room with coolness
and clarity
of blue air

The nocturnal roar
dissolved into tranquility
on the doorstep
colorful leaves

**FALLEN DES WINDES**
*Margret Silvester, Deutschland*

Der sturzbetrunk'ne Wind der Alpen –
Er formt die Hänge und die Täler lässt
Menschen torkeln wie im Rausch; kein Halten
Ist, wenn dieses Kind der Berge mit Lustgeschrei
Gen Boden fällt und meine Seele tränensalzversetzt
Mit Heimweh nur nach Norden an die Küste will.

Der sturzbetrunk'ne Wind der Alpen –

# FALLING WINDS
*Margret Silvester, Germany*

The alpine wind, like total stoned—
shapes mountain ridges, also clefts,
let humans stagger like insane when mountain's
child screams of pleasure and crashes down the slopes
my tear-stained, homesick soul is filled with longings
homebound—to the northern coast.

IL VENTO
*Maria Miraglia, Italia*

Il vento mite stasera
mi accarezza il viso
dolcemente scompiglia i miei capelli

Vorrei essere una foglia
lasciare che il vento mi porti via
sulle sue ali andare
attraverso valli e montagne
traversare gli oceani

Vedere da lontano
le luci delle case
le lampare delle barche in mare
raggiungere una terra remota
per ascoltare la voce del silenzio
e sentirmi tutt'uno con l'immenso

THE WIND
*Maria Miraglia, Italy*

The mild wind tonight
caresses my face
gently ruffles my hair

I'd like to be a leaf
let the wind take me away
on its wings, go
through valleys and mountains
cross the oceans

See from a distance
the lights of the houses
the nightlights of boats at sea
reach a remote land
to hear the voice of silence
and feel one—with the immense

## DO RINGJALLEMI
*Merita Papristo, Shqiperi/Kanada*

Është natë …
Mendimet janë ushqimi
i qeve që flenë në grazhd …
dhe truri ripërtyp dëshirat e pakryera.

Do ringjallemi … ta dish!
Në tjetër kohë në të tjerë trupa
në po këtë botë të egër, të mundimshme, të paditur
si dënim, këtu mes njerëzve
në këtë botë, mbështjellë akoma me egon
që nuk e mposhtëm dot për së pari.
Njëri tjetrin verbërisht
do kërkojmë përsëri, ketu
në udhët që nuk mundëm së bashku t'i shkelnim …

Do ringjallemi dhe do rikërkohemi
Ta dish!
deri sa të gjendemi
si dy pikat fundore të një segmenti
që ethshëm dëshiron të bëhet rreth.

## WE ARE GOING TO REINCARNATE…
*Merita Paparisto, Albania/Canada*

It's night …
Thoughts are the food
of cattle that sleep in the manger …
and the brain is chewing the cud
of yearning desires.

We will reincarnate … mark my words!
At another time, in some other bodies
in the same wild, troublesome, ignorant world
like a punishment,
here among the humans
in this world, still enfolded with the same ego
that we couldn't defeat in the first place …
we are going to look for each other blindly
again, longing to meet
and stepping on all those roads
that we couldn't walk in the first instance.

We will reincarnate
and will re-search for each other …
Mark my words!
until we cling together
as two endpoints of a segment
in its hectic desire to be a circle.

## RÜZGÂRLAR YÜZÜNDE ESİYORSA
*Mesut Şenol, Türkiye*

Gönlünde bir yere yerleşebilme noktasına gelirken
Senin cennetinin arka bahçeleri bir anlaşma arıyor
Yeni gelenler sabreder mi düşlerinde gördükleriyle
Cehennemin bekçilerini aldatmak büyük bir değil yine
de
Ya da bu boşlukta geleceğini tehlikeye atabilirsin
En küçük farklılık için git ve gör ne sunabilirsin
Senin hayatın en engin okyanusların rüzgârlarına
yüzmede

Hiç bitmeyen öykü tam burada, açlık havzasında
başlar
Susuzluk bile bundan sonra saf suyla bile giderilemez
Beynini ve göğsünü kullanmak yüzünü kapatmaya
yetmez
Acımasız bir sevgilinin rüzgârlarından seni hiçbir şey
koruyamaz
Yine de âşıklar, sakin bir meltemin ortasında bir
yerlerde buluşur
Ancak senin kalbinin iklim odasında olan bir şeyler
vardır
İç dünyanda rüzgârlar yüzünde eser eser, hiç durmaz

# IF THE WINDS BLOW ON YOUR FACE
*Mesut Şenol, Turkey*

Coming to fruition in finding a place to settle in your
soul
The back gardens of your own paradise still cry for a
deal
Will the newcomers be patient with what they see in
their dreams?
Again, it's not a huge enterprise to fool the hell's
guards
Or else you might danger your prospect in this
emptiness
See what you can offer in exchange for any subtlety
Your life swims out to reach the vastest ocean' winds

The never-ending story begins just here in the basin of
hunger
Even thirst could not be satisfied by pure water any
longer
Use of the brain or chest will not suffice to cover your
face
Nothing is saved from winds caused by a merciless
lover
Still, lovers meet somewhere in the middle of a calm
breeze
Yet there is something in your climactic heart
chamber
Within your inner world, winds blow on your face
ceaselessly

# SOĞUK RÜZGAR
*Metin Turan, Türkiye*

Yaşlı bir gezegenin konuklarıyız sesini yükseltme,
Bir yere gittiği doğru dünyanın, rüzgar esiyor.

Yaprağa çarptığında kanadı açılıyor kuşların
Su dalgalanıyor halka halka ölü balıklar yayılıyor
etrafa
Sarısı düşüyor yıldızların üşüyorum
Evet, ormanda koyboluyor bir yanım.

Koşuyordum yükünü istiflemiş bir geminin ardından
Kalbimin sana aktığı ırmakta yüzmeyi öğreniyorum
Bir de bulutlar dönüyor başımızda
Saçlarına çarptıkça çoğalan rüzgarımla şehirler
kalabalıklaşıyor
Anlamış olmalısın çiçekleri böyle koklaya koklaya
sana gelişimi
Yorulmuş bir yüzyılın insanıyız
Kalksak düşeceğiz fırtına gözlerimizden belli.

Deniz ve kum gibiyken bakışlarımız
Haykıran rengiyle köpük köpüktür dalgalar
Yıkılır diyordun giderse sesleri
Sen kuşlardan sakın solgun benizli yüzü

Soğumuş süt gibidir zaman
Elin değmişse sokağına evinin
Sıyrılır ağaçlardan dal dal yapraklar
Günboyu usanmadan yağan rüzgardan

Ekmekler soğuk çıkıyor günlerdir
Tuz kokmuş, su kurtlanmış petrol kirine bulanmış
caddeler
Komşu şehirleri de sarmış yalnızlık
Saatin bir gongu daha bozacak sessizliği
Çalışma sürelerini zorlayan dişliler gibi
Acılı bir sesle çiçeklerin sulanmasını öğütlüyor haber
spikerleri
Tuz ve yosun değil mazot ve yorgunluk kokuyor
gemicilerin sohbeti
Yorgunum
Kuytumda kendi rüzgarımla avundum
Nefesim buz kesiği.

THE COLD WIND
*Metin Turan, Turkey*
*Translated by Betül Küre, Turkey*


We are guests of an ancient planet, hush thy voice,
Verily, the world is going somewhere, the wind is
blowing.


As birds brush against a leaf, their wings unfurl
Ripples spread across the water in circles, lifeless fish
scatter around
Stars cast their light, and I shiver with cold
Indeed, a part of me gets lost in the depths of the
forest.


I run behind a burdened ship
Learning to swim in the river where my heart goes
against the tide towards you
And the clouds are swirling above us
With each touch to your hair, my breeze growing,
cities overflow with the crowds
You must have sensed I make my way to you,
savoring the flowers in such a way
We are humans of an exhausted age
Should we rise, we would fall; the storm can be seen
in our eyes.


Like the sea and sand are our looks
The waves are frothy with a resounding hue
You warned of their demise if their voices fade
Protect the paleface from the birds

Time is like cool milk
If your hand touches the streets of your home
Leaves peel off one by one from the trees
Due to the wind ceaselessly descending throughout
the day.

For days on end, the bread comes up cold
Salt has gone stale, water has gone wormy, streets
tainted by the grime of petroleum
Loneliness has embraced the neighboring cities, as
well
Another gong of the clock will disturb the silence
Like gears stretching the limits of working hours
With a painful voice, newsreaders advise watering the
flowers
Not salt and seaweed, but diesel and weariness exude
from the sailors' talks
I am weary
Finding solace in my own breeze in seclusion
My breath is frozen.

# NON SEQUITUR
*Michael Speier, Germany*


vielleicht der wind vielleicht nichts
in den tiefen korbstühlen dieses sterns
nun sind wir angekommen
wo die wildnis begann
als ob sie gewartet hätte
hineingeboren in jene alte sekte
ausgerotteter antlitze
halten wir garantiert durch
rückzug in geduld und zertrümmerte grüfte
wie langbeinige fliegen aus gold

NON SEQUITUR
*Michael Speier, Germany*
*Translated by Richard Dove, Germany*

maybe the wind maybe nothing at all
in the deep wicker chairs
of this star
we've now arrived
where the waste started up
as though it had only been waiting

born into that antique sect
of wiped-out countenances
we'll hold out for sure
(retreat into patience and smashed-up crypts)
like long-legged flies
made of gold

## ЗУБИМА ЗА ВЕТАР УХВАЋЕНА
*Милица Јефтимијевић Лилић, Србија*


„Није да се не усуђујемо јер је тешко,
већ је тешко јер се не усуђујемо!“
Сенека


Не, нисам од оних што чврсто
Приземљени су
И увек знају који је Дан
Колико тешка њихова свака је реч
И који никад не живе свој сан!
Мени је увек потребан Лет,
А имам и танана крила
Што невидљива су
И често кружим орбитом
Иако по земљи ходам
Лакша од своје сенке.

Мени је довољан ветар
Да винем се међ' облаке
Осетим мирис даљина
Што он доноси ми
И само зажмурим,
Хаљином замахнем спретно
Ко играчица фламенка
И зачује се шум.
Полако успињем се
Тамо где носи ме Ум.

Зубима за ветар ухваћена
Заплешем на музику сфера
И све даље сам од ограничења
И зауздаих жеља,
Мргодних лица и злурадих људи.
Слобода испуни сваки душе ми кут
И удишем је жудно, тај озон
Што живот поспешује,
Тај Апсолут,
И не дам да било ко ми суди
Што жудњу слободе имам
Ко птице и пчеле
Та бића сунчана

Што неспутана пењем се изван
Отровних дана
Лака ко звуци далеке харфе
Што сам их Анђео буди.
И топим се у њима, ослобађам
Земаљске чаме, страхова,
Злодела Кројача Света
Што лишише нас сваког смисла.

Спојена с лахором присно
Видим цвили планета препуна Зла
И само што није свисла!

# CAUGHT IN THE WIND WITH TEETH
*Milica Yeftimijević Lilić, Serbia*

> It is not because things are difficult that we do not dare,
> it is because we do not dare that they are difficult.
> *Seneca*

No, I'm not one of those people who are firm.
They are grounded.
And they always know what day it is.
How heavy their every word is.
And who never lives their dream?
I always need to fly,
And I have got thin wings
Because they are invisible
And I orbit often.

Although I walk on the ground
Lighter than my shadow.
The wind is enough for me.
To soar among the clouds
I can smell the distance.
What does it get me?

And I close my eyes,
I'm getting my dress ready.
Like a flamenco dancer
And I heard a noise.
I'm climbing slowly
Where the mind takes me
Caught in the wind with teeth.
I dance to the music of the sphere.

And I'm further away from the limitations.
And bridled desires,
Grim faces and mean people.

Freedom fills every corner of my soul.
And I inhale it eagerly, that ozone
What makes life faster,
That Absolute,
And I don't let anyone judge me.
What a longing for freedom I have
Like birds and honeybees
Those sunny beings.

As unfettered as possible, I climb outside.
Poisonous days
Light as distant harps sound
The Angel who wakes them up.
And I melt in them; I release.
Earthly sorrows, fears,
Atrocities of the Tailor World
Which deprives us of all meaning.

Connected with Lahore intimately
I see a whimpering planet full of evil
And it almost disappeared!

MASUM
*Müberra Karamanoğlu, Türkiye*

Cinayet mahallinden ayrılamayan
katiller gibiyim
Gidemiyorum gönlümden
hep bir korku, bir telaş
hala diri mi diye
Durduk yere katil olmadım ben
dilinde şiirin buruk tadıyla
kim ister geceye fırça sallamayı
kim ister düşler krallığının
gönüllü kölesi olmayı

Evet, itiraf ediyorum
ben boğdum yüreğimi ellerimle
Hangimiz katil değiliz ki?
Çocuk olamamış büyükler
büyütülmemiş çocuklardan ibaretse
bu topraklar
herkesin eli kana bulanmış demektir
Bir de esrik gecelerde
bulamıyorsa düşler yolunu
Aşk da bandırılmışsa günaha
Umut da gelemeyen yolcuysa hep
Kan kokan toprağımda
Ben masumum,
ben masumum aslında.

## INNOCENT
*Muberra Karamanoglu, Turkey*

I'm like killers who cannot leave the crime scene
My heart doesn't let me go
Always a fear
a flurry
Is it still alive?
I didn't become a murderer suddenly
With the acrid taste of poetry.
Who wants to shake a brush in the night?
Who wants to be a slave of the kingdom of dreams
voluntarily?

Yes, I admit
I strangled my heart with my bare hands.
Which of us are not murderers?
If this land is made up of children who are not let
grow up,
Seniors who could not become a child.
Means everyone's hands are covered in blood
And on ecstatic nights
If dreams cannot find their way,
If love is dipped in temptation
If hope is the passenger who may not come, inevitably
In my land that smells of blood
I am innocent
I'm innocent, actually.

UNTAMEABLE
*Neelam Saxena Chandra, India*

Winds, having a mind of their own,
Don't follow the directions you wish they did!
They merrily wander
Amidst the fields,
Enjoying the deserts,
Diving above the seas!

Winds aren't like beings
That can be disciplined;
They are unashamedly untamable.

How much like a woman
Having a mind of her own!

Don't try to control the winds,
They can ransack cities with mammoth structures,
If you try to alter their paths!

WHERE TO GO?
*Neelam Saxena Chandra, India*

He asked me,
"What's the difference between
People who go with the wind
And those who don't?"

I replied with a smile,
"Look at Rama,
He went with the winds, questioning
The chastity of his own wife,
For whom he had fought a whole battle,
Causing a bloodshed!"
          He looked at me interrogatively.
I continued,
"Now glance at the history of Prince Siddhartha,
Who went against the winds
And became enlightened,
Popularly known as Buddha since eons!"

He questioned,
"Do you mean to say that it is always good
To go against the winds?"

I answered,
"Not at all!
I simply wish to say that
One should follow one's own heart
And winds shall have no alternate
Other than to follow you!"

हवा कहाँ जाती है...
पद्मजा अय्यंगार-पैडी, भारत

जब हवा जम कर चलती है,
तब मेरा एड्रिनैलिन दौड़ता है!
हवा के हौले प्रवाह में मैं,
औदात्य अनुभव करती हूँ!


आज़ादी मेरा पसंदीदा परिधान है,
जब मुझे हवा का बुलावा आता है!
उसके कोमल बहाव में मंत्रमुग्ध हो मैं,
खुला महसूस करती हूं, कभी बंधा नहीं!


आज़ादी तब है जब मैं झूमती हूँ,
हवा के प्राकृतिक प्रवाह के साथ!
आज़ादी तब है जब मैं खेलती हूँ,
नर्म और धीमी चलती हवा के साथ!


हवा कभी हबूब का कारण बनती है, तो कभी आँधी का,
कभी सबको गले लगाती है, तो कभी सब कुछ बिखेर देती
है!
हवा कभी हवा है, तो कभी है आँधी,
जीवन की तरह इसके मोड़ - एक अंतहीन कहानी!

हवा कहाँ से आती है और वह कहाँ जाती है?
इसके उतार-चढ़ाव को जानना, कौन न करेगा पसंद?
ठौर-ठिकाने पर खामोश, वह अपनी राह खुद चुनती है;
हवा के अपने रास्ते हैं, किसी की रत्ती भर परवाह नहीं।


हवा के उतार-चढ़ाव से हर्षोन्मत्त हो मैं वाह कहती हूँ!
और उसकी शक्ति को मैं नतमस्तक प्रणाम करती हूं!

WHERE THE WIND GOES ...
*Padmaja Iyengar-Paddy, India*


When the wind gushes,
My adrenaline rushes!
Softly as the wind blows,
To sublimity, I feel close!


Freedom is my preferred apparel,
when I'm beckoned by the wind,
I'm serenaded by its gentle flow,
Feeling liberated, never pinned!


Freedom's when I sway
With wind's natural flow.
Freedom's when I play
With wind, soft and slow.


At times, wind causes a haboob, and at times, a squall.
At times, it embraces all, and at times, it shatters all!
Sometimes wind is a zephyr, and sometimes a gale!
Like life, its twists and turns—a never-ending tale!

Where does it come from, and where does it go?
Its highs and lows, who wouldn't want to know?
Silent on its whereabouts, it plots its own route.
Wind has its own ways; for none, it cares a hoot.

At its highs and lows, I exult with a "Wow!"
To the power of wind, in supplication, I bow.

زوبعة ـ رائد أنيس الجشي
رائد أنيس الجشي ـ السعودية


تَكتبُ النثريةَ الفوقيةَ
مِنْ علاماتِ الاستفهامِ والتعجُّبِ المتطايرة تُثيرُ زوبعةً
تَمحو نقطةً مِنْ فواصلِ الرّضَا
وأنت تَبحثُ عَنْ جَوهرِ البحث


رحلتك هدفٌ دائمٌ
وارتحالُك حياة


أما وجودك فتَقاذفَ أبدي
وإنقاذ الآخرين
ليس إيقاع بوحك
فالسلام ليس لُغتك في الخطاب


.. لا ليفلَّ رمزك .. تَعْقده
بل ليُدركَ الآخرُ
قدرتَه على فضح شفافية العقدة
تسلسل القص وفكِّ رباط


الشمس ـ خدعة القمر الوحيدة ـ
تُجيدُ التلاعب بعواطف الغروب
وحين تُصنَعُ لوحًا
حديثًا تَكسرُ لوحًا


ما زالَ الملح جسدك
وأضلاعك قابلة للاستبدال بمنثور جديد
أو قنينة سرد عتيق
...

WHIRLWIND
*Raed Anis Al-Jishi, Saudi Arabia*

You write superscript prose.
It stirs up a whirlwind of flying question marks and
amazement.
Erase a point from contentment's commas
while you are searching for the essence of the search.
Your journey is a permanent goal,
your peregrinations a life.
As for your existence, it is an eternal toss.
Saving others
is not the beat of your soul
because peace is not your language
in speech.
You knot your symbol, not to be deciphered
but for the other to realize
his ability to expose the transparency of the knot
and untying the sequence bond of recitation.
The sun—the moon's only trick—
is good at manipulating the emotions of the sunset.
And when it makes a tablet,
it breaks a fresh one.
Salt is still your body,
and your ribs could be replaced with a new prism
or a vintage bottle of narration.

## WIND CHIMES
*Reshma Ramesh, India*

If you ever wonder why
I wear the wind around my ankles,
Why I break every sentence into a cyclone or a cloud,
Why I leave little bits of me around you.
It is only to open the door and let the rain in,
To climb into your eyes and look for glass pieces,
Kaleidoscope, breaking hearts and
An unwritten poem
And it is because you asked me not to speak of
Love and language
Not to speak about us
I might as well break them into tamarind seeds.
And sow them here and there,
Perhaps when the night falls, they might grow roots.
And slip into noisy crickets and windchimes
To tell you all about me,
And maybe you would listen
Only if you were an insomniac.

MIGRATION
*Reshma Ramesh, India*

I have waited for the shadows to fill
This land and my tiny palms,
The sky awaits like an expectant mother
For the fluttering birds to fill her womb
For a minute, only to fly away
To fly away beyond the northern lands
Beyond the mighty Himalayas
Where only the snow had found mercy
And the air is packed with knives.
To fly away to meet the eastern gale
Beyond the sliding desert sands
Echoing of Arabic prayers and camel bells
In my garden waits sweet spring
Song-laden flowers and silver snails
Coconut trees and half naked-children
who know nothing about flights.
I have waited for poetry to come to me
Just like the howling winds, making a noise
Awaiting your arrival, bleak-eyed, hungry
But filled with a heart of hope and stories of
Three continents that only your eyes can tell.

# A CURIOUS WIND TO SOOTHE
*Sitawa Namwalie, Kenya*


A curious wind unsettled the stories crowding my
past,
Upset, they were scattered pebbles arranged in a
pattern coherent only to me.
All my poor choices pointed a reproaching finger at
me.
Self-regard, prompting the hatred of others,
Fear saw me stay too long, too long, too late,
Greed had me stray again and again.
Lost in my humanity, I no longer saw the gifts
bequeathed to me.
But the wind is gentle.
It comes to soothe.
Be comforted.
It whispers in stillness,
Your worst is behind you,
Just keep your eyes wide open.

THE COMING OF AN ILL WIND OR SHARING
A WORLD WITH HUMANS WHO WILL
NOT SHARE
*Sitawa Namwalie, Kenya*

Imagine being an elephant and seeing the world as
elephants see, as elephants have seen for millions of
years,

Or a Giraffe staring out into the horizon,
The same horizon their ancestors saw as their necks
began to stretch.

Imagine being a zebra, head down, chewing, chewing,
to keep your rump plump, I suppose?

And then, good grief, here come the humans again,
Like an ill-wind bringing their doom and gloom with
them,

This time, it's a gale force wind threatening to end
your world, oh mighty elephant, oh graceful Giraffe,
oh ever plump zebra.

Just as it did 100 years ago, just as they tried 300 years ago (but that time you prevailed).

It is clear what humans want.
This land is theirs and theirs alone; they will not share.

This time, they come to build everlasting testaments to your exclusion, oh mighty elephant, oh graceful Giraffe, oh ever plump zebra.

Don't worry, oh ancient rhino, the humans will weep every time one of you dies.

This time, the humans build concrete pillars, holding up colossal concrete walls that are sure to live forever.

They pile up the soil, make mountains with inclines so steep, they will break the legs of a baby gazelle too new, too frisky to know, her future is already doomed.

And to ramp up the danger, oh mighty elephant, oh graceful Giraffe, oh ever plump zebra,

Atop these concrete pillars, concrete walls, and steep mountains, a great train rumbles day and night across the landscape.

But pretenses must be maintained, after all, the human
is the most intelligent being on all the earth.

So, every so often,
You will find,
A small passage,
In their new concrete monstrosity.

What is it for?

ENTBLÄTTERT
*Susanna Piontek, USA*

Der Herbst zieht übers Land,
im Schlepptau Geselle Wind,
der das Vorrecht hat,
die Bäume zu entblättern.
Erst umschmeichelt er sie nur milde
und kokett lassen sie
das eine oder andere Blatt fallen.
Kaum aber wird er zudringlicher
und nähert sich ihnen kraftvoll,
erröten die Blätter vor Scham
und klammern sich umso stärker
an ihre Zweige.
Als ihnen bewusst wird:
dieser Kampf ist verloren,
werden sie bleich vor Entsetzen
und segeln ergeben und traurig zu Boden.
Zumindest in Baumnähe wollen sie bleiben,
sind doch Stamm und Wurzeln Vater und Mutter.
Und so wispern sie mit ihren
hinabgewehten Schicksalsgenossen,
sich gegenseitig Zusammenhalt versichernd.

Der Wind lauscht belustigt,
und ohne Erbarmen
wirbelt er sie kraftvoll auf,
reißt Geschwister auseinander
und zwingt zu neuen Banden.
Entkräftet und verdorrend liegen sie schließlich
einzeln oder aneinandergeschmiegt
und nähren im Zerfall neues Leben.

DEFOLIATED
*Susanna Piontek, USA*

Autumn moves across the country,
in tow with wind, his fellow,
who has the privilege
to defoliate the trees.
First, he caresses them only mildly
and coquettishly, they let
the one or other leaf fall.
But no sooner does he become more intrusive
and approaches them forcefully,
the leaves blush with shame
and cling more strongly
to their branches.
When they realize that
this fight is lost,
they turn pale with horror
and sail sadly to the ground.
At least they want to stay close to the tree,
for trunk and roots are father and mother.
And so, they whisper with their
ill-fated comrades who have been blown down,
assuring each other of solidarity.

The wind listens with amusement,
and without mercy
it whirls them up powerfully,
tearing brothers and sisters apart
And forcing new bonds.
Debilitated and withering, they lie at last
alone or nestled together
and, in decay, nourish new life.

REQUIEM
*Utz Rachowski, Deutschland*

Die Liebe
die vielleicht gewaltigste Energie des Menschen
wohin geht sie hin, wo bleibt sie?
Eine der großen Fragen
meines Lebens


Orte: In einigen tausend Jahren soll es
kein menschliches Leben mehr auf der Erde geben


Überleben werden fischähnliche Kreaturen
Silberfische
mit dem Aussehen mittelalterlicher Rittermasken
ihr Unterteil Tentakeln
hinzu kommen perfekt angepasste Tausendfüßler
von ungeheurer Größe


Orte: Ich stelle mir einen solchen vor
wie ein loses Gedichtblatt von einem galaktischen
        Wind
an das Bein eines dieser Tausendfüßler geweht
        wird
und sich dort verfängt

Auf der flatternden Seite steht
ein Gedicht
unter meinem Namen
es ist ein Liebesgedicht

Das muss uns genügen, dass wir gelebt haben
an verschiedenen Orten und Zeugnis gegeben
mit dem TROTZDEM der Liebe:

Wir waren die mit dem flatternden Herzen

# REQUIEM
*Utz Rachowski, Germany*
*Translated by Louise E. Stoehr, USA*

Love
Perhaps the most powerful human energy
where does it go, where does it abide?
One of the great questions
of my life

Places: In several thousand years
human life should no longer exist on Earth

Surviving will be fish-like creatures
silverfish
with the appearance of medieval knights' masks
their lower sections tentacles
to that, add perfectly adapted millipedes
of enormous size

Places: I imagine such a one
like a single page of poetry being blown by
a galactic wind around the leg of one of these
millipedes
and getting entangled there

On this fluttering page, there is
a poem
below my name
it is a love poem

It must satisfy us that we have lived
in various places and born witness
with our NEVERTHELESS of love,

We were those with the fluttering hearts

DER ERSTE TAG
*Uwe Friesel, Deutschland*

Es kommt der Tag
        an dem wir leben
        an dem wir nicht mehr leiden
        an dem wir Menschen sind

Es kommt der Tag
an dem wir neue Lieder dichten
an dem wir hier auf Erden schon
das Himmelreich errichten
an dem wir Menschen sind

Es kommt der Tag
        an dem wir miteinander leben
        wie am ersten Tag

Denn es wird der erste Tag sein

Oder wir werden nicht sein

# THE VERY FIRST DAY
*Uwe Friesel, Germany*

The day will come
>     when we all shall live
>     and suffer no more

The day will come
when a better song
will be our aim
when here on earth,
we shall heaven proclaim
and be humane

The day will come
>     when we live together
>     as on the very first day

Because it will be the very first day

Or we shall not be

પવન સાથે ઊડવું છે મને
*વર્ષા દાસ, ભારત*

હું હંમેશા પ્રેમમાં પડું
ને પછી બહાર નીકળી જાઉં.
એક દિવસ એમ થયું કે
પડવાને બદલે ઊંચે કાં ન ચડું !
પણ ઊંચે ચડીને જાઉં ક્યાં ?
ના, આકાશમાં નહીં,
પહાડો પર નહીં,
વૃક્ષોની ટોચ પર પણ નહીં,
પણ ઊંચે તો જવું હતું.
ત્યાં તો બે પાંખો ઊગી આવી,
પ્રસરી અને ફડફડી,
ઊડવા માટે તૈયાર.
હું પવન સાથે ઊડીશ.
ઉગમણે કે પછી આથમણે,
પૃથ્વીની ફૂદરડીના સથવારે.
એ ઉડ્ડયન મુક્ત અને સુગંધિત,
શાંત અને આનંદિત.

પૃથ્વી પરના પંચ મહાભૂતોમાં

170

એક છે હવા.
એ વહે તો પવન, ને ક્રોધે ચડે તો વાવાઝોડું!
મને બધા જ પવનો ગમે,
શ્વાસ લેવાનું સહેલું બને.

મારું સ્મિત રેલાય ને
સહુને આવરી લે,
મને ઊંચે જવું ગમે
પવન સાથે ઊડવું છે મને.

# GOING WITH THE WIND
*Varsha Das, India*

I was always falling
In and out of love.
One day, I thought,
How about rising in love?
Rise and go where?
Not in the sky,
Not on the mountains,
Not on the treetops,
Yet I wanted to rise.
I saw two wings grow,
Spread and flutter,
Ready to take off.
I will fly with the wind.
To the East or West
As the earth rotates.
It is free and fragrant,
Peaceful and pleasant.

Air, one of the five elements
It is what's on the earth.
When in motion, it is the wind.
And when in fury, it is the typhoon!
I love the wind in all its forms.
It helps me breathe.
My smile spreads,
It embraces all.
I love to rise
And go with the wind.

ΤΗΣ ΣΕΛΗΝΗΣ
*Γιώργος Χουλιάρας*

Αφού εκεί πάνω άνεμος δεν φυσά
σύννεφα δεν υπάρχουν
ποτέ δεν σβήνονται
στη σκόνη τα σημάδια


## OF THE MOON
*Yiorgos Chouliaras, Greece*

As no wind blows up there
and clouds do not exist
there is never any erasure
of the signs in the dust

## YUGO Y ESTRELLA*
*Yuray Tolentino Hevia, Cuba*

Cómo el espantapájaros
aprendí a soportar el sol y amar la libertad del viento
y de las aves.

Aprendí a mezclar, lágrimas con la lluvia
para callar el dolor y a no bajar la cabeza
ni aunque le dieran tirones a mi ropa.

Un día mi corazón tuvo el estruendo
del cañón de trapo de los mambises
y supe entonces que detrás de la montaña
había otra vida donde podía ser libre y enterrar los
miedos.

Y corrí tras la luz de la estrella que ilumina y mata
dejando en la guardarraya el yugo que mancha y
embrutece

* Yugo y Estrella es el título de un poema escrito por el Héroe
Nacional Cubano: José Martí. Incluido en los Versos Libres. Libro
escrito cuando el Apóstol tenía 25 años en 1878.

YOKE AND STAR*
*Yuray Tolentino Hevia, Cuba*
*Translated by Leidy Díaz Hevia, Cuba*

How the scarecrow
I learned to bear the sun and love the freedom of the
wind
and of the birds.

I learned to mix tears with the rain
to silence the pain and not lower your head
Not even if they tugged at my clothes.

One day, my heart had the thunder
from the rag cannon of the mambises
and I knew then that behind the mountain
There was another life where he could be free and
bury his fears.

And I ran after the light of the star that illuminates and
kills
leaving in the guardrail the yoke that stains and
brutalizes.

---

* "Yoke and Star" is the title of a poem written by the Cuba National Hero, José Martí, included in the *Free Verses*—a book written when the Apostle was 25 years old in 1878.

# WO DER WIND WEHT
*Zorin Diaconescu, Rumänien*

wo der Wind weht
sind Sandstürme in Kauf zu nehmen,
dort gibt es volle Segel
und harte Gesichter
Windstille ist kein Traum,
sondern Verhängnis
wo der Wind weht
lernt man Zelte fest verankern,
man baut Windmühlen und
nachts träumen Dichter von Segeln
dort sind Flug und Absturz möglich,
wo der Wind weht gibt es Atmosphäre
also leben dort Menschen
und deshalb haben wir ein Problem
oder auch nicht
doch egal ob der Wind weht oder nicht,
der Bestand der Sandkörner
wird dabei nicht beeinflusst

# WHERE THE WIND BLOWS
*Zorin Diaconescu, Romania*

where the wind blows
sandstorms have to be taken into account,
there are full sails there
and hard faces
calm wind is not a dream,
but doom
where the wind blows
you learn to anchor tents firmly,
you build windmills and
at night, poets dream of sailing
flying and crashing are possible there,
where the wind blows, there is the atmosphere
so people live there
and that's why we have a problem
or not at all
no matter whether the wind blows or not,
the inventory of the grains of sand
is not affected

# Biographies

Achim Amme is an author, actor, and singer-songwriter. He wrote his first songs in English at the age of 15. After a one-year stay as an exchange student in the USA, he studied theater, philosophy, and German studies before receiving his diploma as an actor from the Max Reinhardt School, Berlin, in 1972 and working for several years in the theater (with George Tabori, a. o.)—freelance writer since 1978. Since 1997, he has appeared in films and well-known television series. He has published poems, stories, a biography about his grandfather, and his songs on records and CDs. He is on the road as a reciter with programs on Joachim Ringelnatz and John Lennon, a.o. Various literary prizes and scholarships.

Birgit Funk, translator, is a former teacher of English in Germany and of German in Australia. Now, she works as an editor for German literature.

Agron Shele started his journey in literature when he was very young. He is the author of several novels and poetry books in Albanian language, English language, and other languages as well. Agron Shele is also the coordinator of several International Anthologies. He is the winner of some international literary prizes and a member of the Albanian Association of Writers, member of the World Writers Association in Ohio, USA, Poetas del Mundo, WPS, Union World Poetry, and the President of the International Poetical Galaxy "Atunis." Currently, he resides in Belgium and continues to dedicate his time and efforts to publishing literary works with universal values.

Merita Paparisto, the translator, please see her poet's biography.

Albrecht Classen, University Distinguished Professor of German Studies at the University of Arizona, is the author of ten volumes of his poetry in German and English and of four volumes of satires and essays. He served as book review editor of the literary journal Trans-Lit and is currently the president of the Society for Contemporary American Literature in German (SCALG). In his research, he focuses on the European Middle Ages (124 books currently). In 2004, he received the Bundesverdienstkreuz am Band, and in 2017, the title of Grand Knight of the Most Noble Order of the Three Lions was bestowed upon him.

Ali Alhazmib is born in Damadd, Saudi Arabia. He obtained a degree in Arabic Language and Literature at Umm Al-Qura University, Faculty of

Arabic Language. As early as 1985, Ali started publishing his poetry in various local and Arabic international cultural publications. He has participated in multiple International Poetry Festivals, his work has been translated into many languages, and he has several international awards.

Alicja Maria Kuberska (1960)—awarded Polish poet, novelist, journalist, editor, translator, edited volumes and anthologies in Polish and English. Her poems have been published in numerous anthologies and magazines in Poland and abroad. She is a member of the Polish Writers Associations in Warsaw (Poland) and IWA Bogdani (Albania). She is also a member of the directors' board of Our Poetry Archive (India) and a Cultural Ambassador of The Inner Child Press (the USA).

Anna Würth is an author and photographic artist in Hamburg. Her poems and short stories have been published in 89 anthologies, and her book Aphrodite.Lovestoned. In 2001, she received the Literary Sponsorship Award of GEDOK. She regularly gives public readings both in Germany and abroad. In her Literary Pictures, she combines her poems with her photography. She has exhibited it in Hamburg, Denmark, and Paphos, Cyprus.

John Waterfield, translator, doctorate in classics and English literature at Christ Church, Oxford. Translation of Rainer Marie Rilke's The Duino Elegies, E. Mellen Press. Author of The Heart of His Mystery: Shakespeare and the Catholic Faith in England under Elizabeth and James.

Annabel Villar, poet and cultural activist. Founding member of Liceo Poetico de Benidorm; Associate Academic and Honorary Member American Academy of Modern Literature. Director of "Azul" Poetry Collection and International Poetry Festival "Benidorm & Costa Blanca." Founding Member Student Academy of Contemporary Art (Rio de Janeiro, Brazil, Chair No. 6 "Gabriela Mistral.
Translator: Janine Troutman, the translator, please see her poet's biography.

Antje Stehn, Germany, resides in Italy. Poet, visual artist, art curator, member of German PEN Center German-Speaking Authors Abroad, co-editor of the poetry magazine TamTamBumBum, Los Ablucionistas and Teerandaz. She is a member of the direction committee of the Piccolo Museo della Poesia of Piacenza, Italy. In 2022, she published her most recent bilingual book, Grotesk, by Verlag Expeditionen. Her poems are translated into twelve languages and published in numerous international

Anthologies. Since 2020, she has been curating the art-poetry project "Rucksack A Global Poetry Patchwork," which involves more than 250 international poets.
Betty Gilmore, USA, the translator, please see her poet's biography.

Aristea Papalexandrou was born in Hamburg in 1970 and has studied music and Medieval and Modern Greek Literature and works as an editor. She has published six books of poetry. For her book, It's Passing Us By, she was honored by the Academy of Athens in December 2017.
Philip Ramp, a translator born in Michigan, is a poet and experienced translator who has lived and worked in Greece for over thirty-five years. He has published numerous volumes of original poetry and done many translations from the Greek.

Ayeshah Émon is a poet, academic, educator, and performance artist. She writes in English, Urdu, and French. Her writings cover various subjects about the human condition, such as love, desire, resilience, migration, and belonging.

Barry Stevenson wrote his first poem at 13, his second at 15, and then, from 17 on, he doesn't know how many. When he was 47, a rarely-heard, fearless inner voice told him that, good or bad, he was, always had been, and always would be a poet, and whether he liked it or not or ever composed another line was irrelevant — "it's what you are, so just get on with it ." All this in a split second. So, he did. The result was The Western Park and Tigertale (still in the making) with, in all, some 200-odd satellites in tow.

Betty Gilmore, USA, poet and blues singer, born in Oklahoma and raised in Los Angeles. After studies in Latin American culture at UCLA and teaching in Costa Rica, pursues a career as singer. Begins writing poetry in the '80's, after studies at the Feminist Studio Workshop under graphic artist Sheila De Bretteville and begins performances combining poetry and music. Her work is often designed to raise awareness of African-American, and other marginalized cultures. She has published poems, articles and music over the last 30 years. She currently lives in Milan where she is a member of the multi-cultural poetry collective, Poetry is My Passion.

Bill Wolak is a poet, collage artist, and photographer who lives in New Jersey and has just published his eighteenth book of poetry entitled *All the Wind's Unfinished Kisses* with Ekstasis Editions. His most recent translation with Mahmood Karimi-Hakak, *Love Me More Than the Others: Selected Poetry or Iraj Mirza*, was published in 2014 by Cross-Cultural Communications. His artworks have appeared in different international festivals. He was a featured artist in the book *Best of Erotic Art* (London, 2022).

Chloe Koutsoumpeli has written ten collections of poetry, three novels, and two theatrical plays. She has participated in many Greek and foreign anthologies and festivals of poetry, and her poems and short stories have been published in Greek and foreign magazines. Her collection of poems with the title Those Who Eat at the Same Table in Another Land won the National Award for Poetry in 2016.

Christopher Okemwa is a literature lecturer at Kisii University, Kenya. He has a PhD in performance poetry from Moi University, Kenya. He is the founder and current director of the Kistrech International Poetry Festival in Kenya. His novella, Sabina and the Mystery of the Ogre won the Canadian Burt Award for African Literature in 2015. Its sequel, Sabina the Rain Girl, was selected for the UN SDG 2 Zero Hunger reading list. Okemwa is the editor of four international anthologies recently Ukraine: A World Anthology of Poems on War. He has written ten books of poetry, ten folktales of the Abagusii people of Kenya, four children's storybooks, one play, two novels, and four oral literature textbooks.

Claudia Piccinno is a teacher, poet, and translator. She was born in Lecce and lives in Castel Maggiore near Bologna, where she received a civic award for cultural merit. Her books have been translated into English, Spanish, Serbian, Turkish, French, Arabic, Polish, Macedonian and German. She won prestigious national and international awards and published 50 poetry collections in various languages. The latest in Italy was published by Fara editore in 2023 and is entitled Implicita missione. She is the editor of the Istanbul Gazette and the Turkish magazine Papirus, collaborates with various literary magazines, and is on several juries of national and international poetry competitions. She holds seminars and conferences on the pedagogical value of poetry, the latest at the Catholic University of Milan on May 2023 for theology students in the ethics of communication course.

Daniel Calabrese is an Argentine poet born in Dolores, province of Buenos Aires, who lives in Chile. He has been awarded several international prizes. His books of poetry and anthologies have been published in more than ten countries, and part of his work has been translated into Italian, English, French, Portuguese, Bulgarian, Chinese, and Japanese. He is the founder and director of Ærea, Revista Hispanoamericana de Poesía, and a member of the International Council of the Vicente Huidobro Foundation.

Katherine M. Hedeen is a translator of poetry, literary critic, and essayist. A specialist in Latin American poetry, she has translated some of the most respected voices from the region. She is the Associate Editor for Action Books and the Poetry in Translation Editor at the Kenyon Review. She resides in Gambier, Ohio, where she is a Professor of Spanish at Kenyon College.

Dimitris P. Kraniotis was born in 1966 in the Larissa Prefecture in central Greece and grew up in Stomio (Larissa). He studied Medicine at the Aristotle University of Thessaloniki, lives in Larissa, and works as an internist. He is the author of ten poetry books. His poems have been translated into 34 languages, and he participated in several international poetry festivals. He is a Doctor of Literature, Academician, President of the 22nd World Congress of Poets (UPLI), President of the World Poets Society (WPS), Director of the Mediterranean Poetry Festival (Larissa, Greece), and Chairman of the Writers for Peace Committee of PEN Greece.

Don Krieger is a biomedical researcher whose focus is the electric activity within the brain. He authorizes the 2020 hybrid collection Discovery, the 2022 hybrid chapbook When Danger Is Past, Who Remembers? and is a 2020 Pushcart nominee and a 2020 Creative Nonfiction Foundation Science-as-Story Fellow. His work has appeared in several magazines and was translated into Farsi, Greek, Italian, German, Turkish, Romanian, and Portuguese.

Elçin Sevgi Suçin was born in Denizli, Turkey in 1972. Her poems and articles on poetry appeared in various literary magazines. She published two poetry collections in Turkish. Her third and fourth collections are under publication. Some of her poems have been translated into English, German, Italian, Arabic, and Persian. She lives in Ankara, Turkey.

Emel Koşar was born in Eskişehir (1981). In 2003, she graduated from the Turkish Language and Literature Department of the Faculty of Arts and Sciences of Mimar Sinan University of Fine Arts. She is currently a faculty member at the Turkish

Language and Literature Department of the Faculty of Arts and Sciences of Mimar Sinan University of Fine Arts. She has published her poetry and essays on Turkish literature in various literary magazines. She published her research and reviewed books, scientific and literary works, and eight poetry collections.

Yaprak Damla Yıldırım , the translator, was born in 1994. She graduated from Boğaziçi University Management and Western Languages and Literatures departments in 2017. In March 2015, she was appointed as "The Young Poet" by Yasakmeyve and got two awards for her poetry collections.

Emina Čabaravdić-Kamber is a poet, author, painter, and VHS lecturer for exile literature & art in Hamburg, Lübeck, Münster, and Bosnia and Herzegovina. Born in the central Bosnian town of Kakanj, she was the only one of eleven children to leave her home in 1968. She founded the International Literary Club "La Bohemina" in 1988 and has published multilingual books and was awarded several literary prizes.

In 1996, she was awarded the Medal of Merit of the Order of Merit of the Federal Republic of Germany by President Roman Herzog for her literary work on

peace and ending the war in Bosnia and Herzegovina.
Gino Leineweber, the translator, please see his poet's biography.

Evangelia Liana Sakelliou is a poet, translator, critic, editor, and university professor from Athens, Greece. She is the author of twenty-six books, most recently: Murmullo (Selected Poems, Sevilla, Padilla Libros 2023), Eva: The Voices of an Imaginary Poet (Translations of Aliki Barnstone's Eva's Voice, Vakhikon, 2023), Portrait Before Dark (poetry collection, San Antonio Texas: St. Julian Press, 2022). Her poems have been translated into ten languages and widely anthologized.

George Wallace is a writer in residence at the Walt Whitman Birthplace, author of 40 chapbooks of poetry, and editor/co-editor of Great Weather for Media, Poetrybay, and From the Inside – An Anthology of NYC Poetry. George travels internationally to share his work, receives top honors at festivals in Europe, Asia, and South America, and this year released poetry/music collaborations in NYC and Athens, Greece. He is the founder and manager of Poets Building Bridges, an international triangulation of poets through Zoom.

Gino Leineweber was born in 1944 and has been working as a poet, writer, and translator since 1998. He lives in Vietri sul Mare, Italy, and Hamburg, Germany. He led the Hamburg Authors' Association for twelve years and was appointed honorary chairman in 2015.
From 2013 to 2020, he was president of the Three Seas Writers' and Translators' Council, based in Rhodes, Greece. He is currently a board member of the PEN Center German-Speaking Authors Abroad (formerly German Exile PEN).
He writes in German and American English; since 2016, he has translated prose and poetry from English.
Barry Stevenson, the translator, please see his poet's biography.


Hema Ravi is a part-time IELTS and Communicative English trainer and writer by passion. She is a prize winner in short story and poetry competitions. Working as the Secretary of the Chennai Poets' Circle (CPC) and editor of 'Efflorescence,' the anthology of CPC. As Secretary of Connecting Across Borders (CAB), she organizes international poetry seminars and panel discussions. A resource person for workshops, she is also an independent researcher.


Hilal Karahan is a Turkish poet, writer, translator, mother, and medical doctor. She was born in 1977 in Gaziantep/Turkey. She has been writing professionally since 2000 and has joined many collective books and bilingual poetry almanacs and found on the organization committee of international poetry festivals. She has six poetry books, three prose books, and many selected poems published in different languages. She is a member of Turkey PEN, intercontinental director of the World Festival of Poetry (WFP), linked by the UNESCO organization, a Turkey member of the World Poetry Movement (WPM), and Turkish ambassador of the World Institute of Peace (WIP). She has organized the International FeminIstanbul Women's Poetry Festival every year since 2016. She has many national and international poetry awards. Since 2017, she has been a member of the publishing council of international bilingual poetry magazines Absent, Rosetta Word Literatura, and Sahitya.

Holly Iglesias' work includes three poetry collections—Souvenirs of Shrunken World, Angles of Approach, and Sleeping Things—and a critical work, Boxing Inside the Box: Women's Prose Poetry. She has received fellowships from the National Endowment for the Arts, the North Carolina Arts Council, and the Massachusetts Cultural Council. Her current projects are Theories of Flight, an intergenerational memoir, and Dear Everybody, 1947, an annotated collection of letters between her mother and friends who had been co-workers during WWII.

Hussein Habasch is a poet from Afrin, Kurdistan, born in 1970. His poems have been translated into over 30 languages and published in over 120 international poetry anthologies. He has about 20 books published in several languages. He participated in many international festivals of poetry, including Colombia, Nicaragua, France, Puerto Rico, Mexico, Germany, Romania, Lithuania, Morocco, Ecuador, El Salvador, Kosovo, Macedonia, Costa Rica, Slovenia, China, Taiwan, New York City, Spain, Greece, and Albania.

Janine Troutman is a lifetime scribbler and linguist, translator, interpreter, and speaker. She worked on a World Bank Project in Beijing and has collaborated, for example, with Pearson Editorial in Spain. Hitherto, an undercover poet, she versified in Spanish, English, and French and has a penchant for speaking in other people's voices, telling other people's stories, tall or not.
She makes frequent forays to the heights of the flat-topped Swabian Alps to achieve a more global worldview in her calling as a coolly impassioned,

radically uncensored chronicler of current considerations, both in and out of rhyme.

Jenny Lkhagvasuren started writing poems in 2013. Some of her poems have been published in the Illinois State in the USA, Turkey, Italy, Albany, Germany, and India in poetry anthologies. In addition to writing poems, Jenny has translated many of the world's best literary, educational, and children's books from English to Mongolian and has been published since 2019.

Jeton Kelmendi, born in 1978 in Peja, Kosovo, is a poet, player, publicist, translator, publisher, university professor, academic, and active member of the European Academy of Science and Arts in Salzburg, Austria. He has published eleven poetry books, twelve books in science politics, and translated 70 books and two plays. He is the most translated Albanian poet. Actually, he works as a professor at AAB University College in Pristina, as he lectures at different universities in Europe and the USA. Kelmendi is considered a poet who writes lyrics with strong imagination and elliptic verses.

Julio Pavanetti is a poet and a cultural promoter. He is the president of the int'l Poet's Association Liceo Poético de Benidorm, an Honorary Member of the

North American Academy of Modern Literature, Director of the Benidorm International Poetry Festival, and a Member of the Spanish Writers and Artists Association. He has published fourteen poetry books. He has received many international awards. He has participated in several poetry festivals and more than 100 anthologies. Many of his poems have been translated into 27 languages.

Kirsten Döbler studied Russian, English, and Educational Sciences at Hamburg University. She began her literary activities in 2005, inspired by impressions she gained during her professional collaboration with Russian partner organizations in education and tourism. Initially, she wrote short stories and tales, but soon, her thematic and genre range broadened, and she composed genre novels. In recent years, her focus has been on poetry.

Lily Exarchopoulou was born in Athens in 1959 and still lives there. She has studied UK Ancient History and Archaeology as well in Greece, English, and American Literature, and returned to the U.K. for her M.A. in the 19th and 20th Century Novels. She has worked as a teacher of English, Ancient History, and European Literature, a journalist, a translator, and a book reviewer. She has published three novels, three poetry books, and numerous short stories in anthologies, newspapers, and magazines. She still hopes for a more inclusive world and loves Art and the Sea.

Maja Herman-Sekulić is a Serbian author of 24 books translated into 27 languages. Of her, Nobel laureate Joseph Brodsky said: "Her poetry is of the rarest talent and beauty as she is herself ." Maja is an internationally acclaimed poet, novelist, essayist, bilingual scholar, and a significant translator. She is also a Vice President of the International Ethics Academy based in India. Her latest novel, Nine Lives of Milena Pavlovic Barillli, published in Serbian and English in 2021 and in Italian, translated by Claudia Piccinno, was awarded "Best foreign novel" in Italy in 2023. She is also a world traveler and a Princeton Ph.D.

Maren Schönfeld, poetess and journalist. She has five poetry books and two nonfiction books published so far. In 2017, she received the Poetry Award from the Hamburg Authors' Association (Hamburger Autorenvereinigung).
Kirsten Döbler, the translator, please see her poet's biography.
Margret Silvester studied literature at the University Hagen. Her short stories and poems appeared in

anthologies of various publishers. She wrote for a German Broadcast company, a newspaper and was the initiator of the Literature Café. She led the course "Literature and Other Truths". Various Symbiosis exhibitions (text and image) followed in Hamburg and Lower Saxon. She was awarded several prizes and is a member of the German Writers' Union (VS Hamburg) and the Hamburg Authors' Association.

Maria A. Miraglia, a renowned bilingual poet, translator, essayist, and ministerial lecturer for English language teachers, has been an active member of Amnesty International and currently holds the position of President of WFP. Furthermore, she's the Literary Director of the P. Neruda Cultural Association and serves on the editorial boards of numerous international literary and peace organizations. She has published 21 anthologies. Her poems have been translated into 30 languages and featured in over 100 collections and magazines. She has received several international awards and, recently, has been elected a member of the European Academy of Science and Arts in Salzburg.

Merita Paparisto started writing poetry and prose in middle school. Writing is her hobby and her passion. She has published three poetry books in the Albanian language and translated and published a book with short stories from well-known authors. Other poetry written by her and translations have been published in different online magazines or portals. She has also been published in several anthologies in the Albanian language and English.

Mesut Şenol graduated from the Political Science Faculty of Ankara University. His five poetry collections were published, and many of his poetry and literary translations appeared in many national and foreign literary publications and anthologies. He attended several national and international poetry and literary festivals in the country and abroad and acted as an organizer for some of them. He received numerous literary awards in the country and abroad. He is a member of many literary organizations. In May 2016, he was elected to serve on the Executive Board of the Three Seas (Baltic Sea, Black Sea, and the Mediterranean Sea) Writers and Translators Council. He is the Turkey Culture Delegate of the Liceo Poetico De Benidorm based in Spain.

Metin Turan was 1966 born in Kars-Kağızman. He received education in technical training, health, and economics. He entered the literary world through a short story, and the first story was published in 1982. He participated in the Peace Forum organized during the 2018 Winter Olympics in South Korea, and his speech and poems were published in 25 languages.

Michael Speier is a poet, literary scholar, and translator living in Berlin and has taught at the Freie Universität Berlin, the University at Leipzig, and several U.S. universities. He is also an Adjunct Professor at the German Department of the University of Cincinnati and an Honorary Fellow of the AATG. In addition to having published several anthologies and translated modern English, French, and Italian poetry, he is the founding editor of the Paul-Celan-Jahrbuch and the literary magazine Park. He has published twelve volumes of poetry. His work has appeared in over 50 anthologies, has been translated into fourteen languages, and has received several international awards. He is a Member of PEN Germany and of the Académie Mallarmé (Paris).

Richard Dove, the translator, was born in Bath/U.K., and read Modern Languages at Oxford before teaching German and English at Universities in England, Wales, and southern Germany. Now living in Munich, he has published seven collections of poetry (the last six in German) and several editions (e.g., of poems by Michael Hamburger). He has also translated several German-speaking poets into English.

Milica Jeftimijević Lilić graduated from the Faculty of Philosophy in Pristina and won a master's degree in philological sciences at the University of Belgrade, and was a professor at the University of Pristina and editor of Belgrade TV. Milica is an academician of the Slavic Academy in Varna and an honorary Doctor of Literature of the European Institute for Roma Studies, essayist and literary critic, cultural activist and promoter of world literature. She is a member of the Italian Council for Science and Law in Rome, which is part of UNESCO. She has 30 books of poetry, short stories, and essays published and translated into more than 30 languages and was awarded several national and international prices. She was Vice President of the Association of Writers of Serbia and living in Belgrade.

Muberra Karamanoglu is a multidisciplinary artist. She lives in Ankara, Turkey, as a poet, writer, painter, and sculptor. She also performs live performances called "Painting Poems," where she combines poetry and painting. In 2015 her poetry book called Aramıza Şiir Kaçtı/ Poetry Escaped Between Us was published. In 2019, I participated in the International Literature Festival in Bistrita, Romania. Her poems have been translated into English, Romanian, and Spanish.

Neelam Saxena Chandra writes in English and Hindi and has authored six novels and nine short story books, 40 poetry collections, and 15 children's books to her credit. She holds three records with the Limca Book of Records. She has received several awards for her literature.

Padmaja Iyengar-Paddy, formerly a senior banker and an urban governance consultant, is currently the President of Connecting Across Borders and the Vice President of Poetry India International. She has compiled and edited six international multilingual poetry anthologies, of which the Limca Book has recognized Amaravati Poetic Prism 2016 to 2019 as "Poetry Anthology in Most Languages." The India Book of Records has recognized Paddy's poetry collection P-EN-CHANTS for never-before-attempted management subjects and movie reviews in rhyming poetry. P-EN-CHANTS … Again, is her latest poetry collection.

Raed Anis Al-Jishi, an internationally awarded poet and translator from Qateef - Saudi Arabia, has an honorary fellowship in writing from Iowa University,

USA. He is a member of the advisory committee of the exquisite Teacher Training Plan of the national Changua University of Education, Taiwan, and an editor in Modern Dialogs, Northern Macedonia. Some of his books were translated into several languages and won international awards.

Reshma Ramesh is an award-winning bilingual poet writing in English and Kannada. She has the honor of displaying her poem permanently in the ruins of the Ancient City of Olympos, Antalya, Turkey. She has represented India at prestigious international festivals. Her latest book, Language of Shadows, a collection of poetry and photography, is published by Edition Delta Germany. She is a distinction holder in BFA photography, conducted solo exhibitions of her photographs internationally, and practices Dental Surgery in Bangalore, India.

Sitawa Namwalie is an award-winning Kenyan poet, playwright, and performing artist known for her unique dramatized poetry performances, which combine poetry and classical Kenyan musical traditions. Sitawa's growing work includes short stories, dramatized poetry productions, and plays. She is a fellow of the Tallberg Foundation, lives in Nairobi, works as an international consultant, and holds a BSC in Botany and Zoology from the

University of Nairobi and an M.A. in Environmental Studies from Clark University, Massachusetts, USA. In her youth, Sitawa Namwalie represented Kenya in tennis and hockey.

Susanna Piontek writes short stories, poetry, essays, and book reviews. Her first book, Have we possibly met before? And other stories were published in Germany and translated into English, followed by publications in the USA, Austria, Israel, Albania, and Germany. She is a member of the PEN Centre of German-Speaking Writers Abroad, the association "Die Kogge" and of SCALG (Society for Contemporary American Literature in German), from which she received the SCALG Poetry Award (2015) and SCALG Prose Award (2018).

Utz Rachowski was a former political prisoner in East Germany and, as such, was sentenced to 27 months of jail time for five of his poems. He has published 14 books of stories, essays, and poetry. He received several awards for his literature.
Louise E. Stoehr, translator, is a Professor of German at Stephen F. Austin State University in Nacogdoches, Texas. She has published numerous literary translations by authors including Günter Grass, Elfriede Jelenik, Hans-Joachim Schädlich, Sarah Kirsch, and Uwe Kolbe.

Uwe Friesel, having stayed for decades in Italy and Sweden, now lives as a freelance writer near Hamburg, Germany. In the seventies, he founded the AutorenEdition (AE). He has published novels, short stories, poems, children's books, and radio drama. With the historian Walter Grab, he edited a widespread anthology of German political poetry of the 19th Century, Noch ist Deutschland nicht verloren. His German translations of short stories by John Updike and novels by Vladimir Nabokov are noted. He was the co-founder of the International Writers' Centers Visby and Rhodes.

Varsha Das writes in Gujarati, Hindi, and English and translates from Bengali, English, Gujarati, Hindi, Marathi, and Odia. Being born into a family of writers and journalists, she started writing children's stories in Gujarati when she was a teenager. Her first book of children's stories was published when she was 18. She has more than 50 publications in short stories, essays, poems, radio plays, visual art reviews, travelogue, biography, translation of poetry, and books for children. Her latest publications are a collection of her lectures on Mahatma Gandhi and a translation of contemporary Gujarati poems into Hindi.

Yiorgos Chouliaras is a Greek poet, essayist, prose writer, and translator. A former president of the Hellenic Authors' Society, the principal Association of literary writers in Greece, his work has been published in translation in Ploughshares, Poetry, The Harvard Review, and elsewhere.

Yuray Tolentino Hevia is a poet, screenwriter, curator, art critic, and producer. He graduated with a Bachelor of Sociocultural Studies and Art Direction. His work has been published in different magazines, newspapers, and poetry and narrative anthologies in Cuba and abroad. He has published three books and received several international awards.
Leidy Diaz Hevia, the translator, is licensed in a Foreign Language. She has passed several postgraduate courses where she has improved professionally. She has translated poems into English by several poets in different anthologies and international magazines in Belgium, Russia, France, Indonesia, Germany, and Greece.

Zorin Diaconescu only put his literary aspirations into action after retirement. Previously, he was an English teacher and, from the age of 42, a journalist. Both professions influence his writing; he is more of a reporter than a poet. As a layman, he writes what he wants, unlike the professional writer who is forced to write what the reader buys.